Story Numbers

Helpers: Service

1. Dave Nielsen helps his country (military)
2. Bryan Stevenson helps keep the world fair (lawyer)
3. Ruth Bader Ginsburg helps defend the constitution (judge)
4. Michael Tubbs helps his community (politician)
5. Ernie Stevens and Joe Smarro help keep people safe (police officers)
6. Harriet Duren and Chief Rochelle Jones help fight fires (fire fighter)
7. T. Morgan Dixon and Vanessa Garrison help a good cause (non-profit)
8. Joe Madiath helps people get clean water (public health)
9. Beverly Bass helps people travel (pilot)

Helpers: Medical

10. Dr. Bill Magee helps fix smiles (dentist)
11. Dr. Andrew Bastawrous helps improve sight (ophthalmologist)
12. Dr. Pol helps sick animals (veterinarian)
13. Professor Hugh Herr helps people walk (bionic engineer)
14. Andy Puddicombe helps people feel happy (mental health)
15. SIRUM team helps people get medication (pharmaceuticals)
16. Kevin Hazzard helps people in emergencies (ambulance driver)
17. Anushka Naiknaware helps people heal (medical devices)

By Holly A. Sharp

Helpers: Growth

18. Kristina Kuzmic helps her family (parent)
19. Dru Joyce helps his team (coach)
20. Tony Robbins helps motivate (speaker)
21. Sal Khan helps people learn (teacher)
22. Dawn Wacek help readers (librarian)
23. Dave Ramsey helps people get out of debt (money manager)

Helpers: Nature

24. Greta Thunberg helps stand up for the earth (activist)
25. Jane Goodall helps chimpanzees (conservationist)
26. Ann Daag helps giraffes (zoologist)
27. Ocean Ramsey helps sharks (marine biologist)
28. John and Molly Chester help grow food (farmers)

Discoverers

29. Peter Larson looks for dinosaurs (archeologist)
30. Stephanie D. Wilson looks for better ways to go to space (astronaut)
31. Sara Seager looks for aliens (astronomer)
32. Stephen Hawking looks at how space works (physicist)
33. Dr. Mandë Holford looks for cancer cures (chemist)
34. Susie Crate looks for what people can teach us (anthropologist)
35. Kizzmehia Corbet looks for cures to sicknesses (medical researcher)
36. Bill Nye looks for scientific proof (science advocate)
37. Jean Bennett looks for how our bodies work (geneticist)
38. Hannah Fry looks for patterns (data scientist)
39. Pranav Mistry looks for new technology (technologist)
40. Studs Turkel looks for stories (historians)

Dear Dreamers,

What an exciting time to be looking to the future. The world around you is changing faster than it did for your parents or your grandparents. Technology is changing every day, the earth is counting on you, and we are working to be a kinder, more equal human race. You will have a major part in all of that. The question is: what will be your role in this change?

Although these people may have different job titles, they have a few things in common:

1. They didn't just dream about doing something. **They did something about it.**
2. **They didn't wait** until they were a "grownup" to start. They found something they were good at or cared about when they were young and followed it.
3. **They kept going when things were hard**. Many people in this book didn't have easy childhoods or were told they were too different to be successful. They didn't care and let their dreams and hard work lead the way.
4. **They weren't scared of failing**. To do something great means trying. Trying means possibly failing. You may try 99 times and fail, but what if you change the world the 100th time you try?
5. **They cared about the world around them**. It's okay to want to make money. It's okay to want to be famous. It's okay to want to follow a talent you're good at. All of these things just get better when you use your money and talents to improve the world around you as well.

I hope that even just one of these stories makes you curious enough to go out and try something new, explore a talent, or learn more. Each and every one of you has nothing but the future ahead of you and every possibility still remains open, even beyond the 100 in this book. Take advantage of this freedom and explore. Try as much as you can, don't be afraid to fail, and when you find something you love or something you care about, keep doing it.

I would love to hear from you, on social media or by email, about what dreams you have and if you found one in this book.

No matter what, keep dreaming and keep doing.

Holly A. Sharp—author, mother, entrepreneur, brand wizard, inventor, and researcher.

DREAM
IT &
do it
100 POSSIBILITIES,
STORIES,
REAL-LIFE ROLE MODELS.
FOR GIRLS AND BOYS

INSPIRING ALL THE
THINGS YOU CAN BE

HOLLY A. SHARP

Dream of Helping
SERVICE, MEDICAL, GROWTH AND NATURE

Any dream can help others if you use your skills to make a difference.

The careers in this section are the ones you could dream of getting if you're dedicated to making the world a better place.

Service helpers dedicate themselves to serving others. They help keep the world fair, safe, and better than the way they found it.

Medical helpers keep us healthy and help us when we're sick or hurt.

Growth helpers are dedicated to making us better people. They help us grow up, learn lessons, and feel good about ourselves.

Nature helpers study animals and the planet in order to make it better. They stand up for the causes they believe in and give us information to better care for our world.

Helpers rely on their love of people and the planet to be good at what they do.

In whatever way you want to make the world a better place,

Dream it and then Do it.

Dream of Helping Your Country

LIKE

Dave Nielsen

Helping to keep peace around the world and in our country is a job that the United States takes very seriously. America relies on the Navy to keep peace in the waters, the Air Force to keep peace in the air and the Army to keep peace on land.

Dave Nielsen serves with the Army and trains dogs to prepare for missions in foreign countries. The solider and the dog train together and serve together, so an intense bond is formed between the solider and the dog they train.

"This dog taught me so much about how to live a selfless life and serve others," Dave says.

When Dave was introduced to the different dogs he had the option to partner with, he picked out Peppers right away. All the dogs were male except one who was female and smaller than the rest.

"She would tilt her head and I could tell she was thinking and feeling. I don't know why I fell in love with her instantly, but I did. We are trained to not develop feelings for them, but it is hard not to," said Dave about their meeting.

Dave wanted to establish a bond between them, as he knew they were headed to another country together.

They spent hours training together and learning a language that only the two of them spoke. "Most people don't do this, but I taught her the cue to bark. People wondered why, because who would want a dog on a mission to bark? However, I did this because then I could also teach her the cue to be quiet, which is a trait you really want."

They were on a mission together and it was a very dark night.

They were next to a forest and there was a dangerous man hiding in the trees where no one could reach him or see him except for Peppers.

Peppers had been trained for this moment and went into a dangerous situation without hesitation. She saved the lives of the soldiers on the mission but didn't come out of the forest afterwards.

Peppers is remembered as being a great friend and the reason that Dave was able to come home to his daughter.

Serving your country requires you to be very brave and have a desire to make the world a better place.

One thing you can do to make the world a better place is to visit the website www.volunteermatch.org and search in your zip code for volunteer opportunities. You can search for opportunities by the things you are interested in and that are good for kids. There is also an option for virtual volunteer work.

Dream of Helping Keep the World Fair

LIKE

Bryan Stevenson

Have you ever had an argument with one of your siblings where both of you run to your mom or dad to make your case? Who started it? Who was wrong? Who did what to whom? Your mom or dad hears what you have to say, asks questions, trusts you to tell the truth, and then decides who was wrong and how to handle it. You have had a small trial and your parent was the judge and jury.

If a crime is committed, the police try to locate the criminal and arrest them. Similar to the case you make to your parent, there is a trial to decide if the person did the crime or not and how they should be punished.

There are two sets of lawyers at a trial.

The first lawyer shares all the facts from the police officer that made them believe that the person is guilty.

The second lawyer presents the facts that show why that person is innocent. A jury of 12 people listens to both sides and decides who made the better case. A judge listens to everything to make sure the facts are presented fairly.

Bryan Stevenson is a defense lawyer who works for people accused of committing a crime.

When Bryan was a child, a group of lawyers changed his life. There were laws in his community that made it difficult for him to go to college because of the color of his skin. The law changed because of lawyers that came into his community and made it possible for him to go to high school and college. He wanted to keep giving back to communities that are treated differently, like his was.

Sometimes you might get punished for something you didn't do or that didn't happen the way someone said it did. That can also happen to adults. Sometimes those people cannot afford to hire anyone to help prove that they are innocent. Bryan didn't think this was fair, so he started helping people that might be innocent but were called guilty. He formed a group of people to help and they are called the Equal Justice Initiative.

One of the men that Bryan helped was in trouble for hurting another person. The police found fingerprints that they said were the same as the man on trial. He was punished for the crime, but when Bryan and his team took another look at the fingerprints, they didn't match at all.

The people who collected the fingerprints made a mistake and Bryan helped get this man out of jail. There are many people like this that Bryan has helped. He says, "There is a sign over the courtroom that reads 'equal justice for all.' I have to believe that is true."

One way that you can experience the process of going to trial is with the game, "Lawsuit." You can find it on Amazon and it is designed to teach young people about how our legal system works.

Dream of Helping Defend the Constitution

LIKE

Ruth Bader Ginsburg

While the United States has lot of laws, the ideas written in the United States Constitution are considered the most supreme laws. These are things like freedom of speech, which makes sure the government can't prevent you from saying things it might disagree with. The Constitution also makes sure that if you're accused of a crime, you should get to have a trial in court before being found guilty. There are many other laws in the Constitution; each of these laws is critical to the American way of life. The words that Ruth Bader Ginsburg dedicated her life to defending are the first three in the document, "We the people." She was the second woman to serve on the highest court in the United States (the Supreme Court) and she believed that all people, regardless of who you are, should have equal rights.

When she was younger, she was always interested in doing what the boys did. If they were jumping from rooftop to rooftop, well, so was she. This didn't change as she grew older. She observed our government accusing people of things that were unfair and saw that it was their lawyers that gave them a chance to prove their innocence. Because of this, she went to law school where she had to learn to "play with the boys" all over again, as there were very few women in her class.

After law school, it was hard for her to find a job as a woman lawyer, but this did not stop her. She found a job teaching law and her students got her interested in women's rights. She understood how many women felt as she experienced unfairness against women herself. When she was working and pregnant, her boss lowered her pay and her job title because he didn't believe pregnant women should be working. She did not speak up then, but she was determined to create laws that would help women to be treated more like men were treated.

After proving that she was a very good lawyer, who cared about equality, Justice Ginsburg was appointed to be one of nine judges on the Supreme Court of the United States. It is the most important court in our country. They have the final say over how to read the constitution. She said, "If congress passes a law or the president issues an executive order that is in conflict with the Constitution, the Constitution must prevail."

Imagine if you wanted to get a certain type of training or education but weren't allowed to because of your gender. This happened at a military school in Virginia where women were not allowed. The school said it was fair because men train better without women around and women said it wasn't fair because they wanted to get the training too. Justice Ginsburg and almost all the other judges agreed with the women and with the 14th amendment of the Constitution. It was agreed that women must be treated equal.

She would be a part of many cases just like this through her career. Some she would agree with the outcome, and many others she would disagree with the outcome. No matter what, she would continue to fight for the equal rights of all. Because of this, she became one of the most popular and beloved justices of all time—even earning the nickname "the Notorious RBG" after a famous rap star.

She said, "I am eighty four years old and everyone wants to take a picture with me. I just don't take selfies!"

If justice is something that is important to you, the most important place to start is learning about our Constitution. A fun way to learn about this important document is with a game called Constitution Quest (www.constitutionquest.com)

Dream of Helping Your Community

LIKE

Michael Tubbs

Not every school in the United States is the same. When you sit in your classroom, do the number of kids make it easier or harder to pay attention to the teacher? When you go into your school, do you feel safe? When you have trouble understanding what you're learning, is there someone that can give you extra help? Not everyone who goes to public schools can answer these questions in the same way. The people that help us solve these problems, like making our schools better, are our politicians. Politicians also solve problems like safety and jobs.

You don't have to be the President of the United States to make a difference in these areas. In fact, the politicians that work in your neighborhood have a lot to do with the decisions that impact you directly. Michael Tubbs realized this, so at only twenty two years old, he became a politician in his hometown in order to make it a safer and better place to live.

The neighborhood that Michael grew up in wasn't very safe. His mother would try to keep him indoors as much as she could by encouraging him to read or play video games. She says that, "Bookstores were his Disneyland." Michael took the knowledge he learned from reading and wrote essays and learned to debate. In middle school one of his essays won a contest and was published in a famous newspaper. In high school he was a finalist in a debate that was attended by president Obama. Because of all of his hard work, he earned a scholarship to one of the best colleges in the world and was able to leave his difficult neighborhood behind him…or so he thought.

Just before he was getting ready to graduate, he was working as a helper at the White House. One day at work he got a call that his cousin had been hurt by someone in his hometown and all the memories of his childhood came rushing back. He thought, "I could go on and make lots of money for myself and get my family out of this dangerous place, or I can use what I have learned to try and make it better." Michael knew that the best way to make a difference was to be a politician in the part of town he grew up in. There he could help change the laws that made it hard for people to improve their lives. He also knew that he had to get people to vote for him, but he was still a college student and would be one of the youngest people to get voted into a political office in all of America.

But this took work. He gathered anyone he could think of and they walked door to door, living room to living room, and church to church asking for votes and for money in order to beat the man who was in office. Michael thought that the man who was in office didn't look much like his neighbors, didn't understand them, and that he hadn't done much to make his neighborhood safer or better. A lot of high school and college kids came out to help because, even though they couldn't vote, they believed that change was possible. It took a lot of people knocking on a lot of doors, but people started to pay attention.

He was given money from celebrities like Oprah and MC Hammer and making the news for being so young. It worked and he won. He kept his promise and worked to be a good neighbor. Four years later, he asked people to vote for him as Mayor and again, he won, becoming one of the youngest mayors of all time! As Mayor he had this idea that we should pay as much attention to the bullies as we do to those who are being hurt. He believes that bullies might be less likely to hurt people if they think that someone cares for them. Again, he was right and the number of bullies and people being hurt went down. Michael has had lots of different ideas about how he can go back to the golden rule and teach people how to be good neighbors, which you can do whether you're 22 or 82.

Whether it's in your own neighborhood or at a broader level, there are issues that you can get involved in at a young age. Things like: how climate change will impact your generation, how to make schools safer, or how to make all people equal. Find the address for the city council, mayor, congressman, or senator that represents you and let them know how you feel.

15

Dream of Helping Keep People Safe

LIKE

Ernie Stevens and Joe Smarro

If you saw someone at school being picked on or bullied, what would you do? Would you step in and stand up for the person? If you are the type of person that would stand up, say something or help, you might make a great police officer.

Police officers are an important part of our society as they not only help fight crime, but they also help stand up for the people who can't always stand up for themselves, like the kid being bullied on the playground.

Ernie Stevens and Joe Smarro are partners on the San Antonio, Texas police force. Ernie got into public service through being a boy scout. Joe entered public service because he was in the army and wanted to see the world become a better place, especially for children.

When Ernie was a young police officer, he signed up for a class that was about how to handle high-pressure situations. He had no idea what the class was going to be like, but a friend suggested that he take it. During the class, a woman came in and talked about her son who had a mental illness.

She said, "One day you might have to come to my house to help me with my son. I hope if you do that you can do so without it being dangerous."

Mental illness is a disease that causes people to think or behave without normal control. Ernie realized that there was a need for a people who were skilled at working with people who have a mental illness. They needed to be listened to and treated instead of arrested and brought to jail.

Joe says he thinks about a quote from the movie *Avatar* when he meets someone he needs to help. He says, "I see you."

One in five people in the United States have some sort of mental illness, so knowing how to help them is an important part of a police officers' job. Ernie was able to start a unit in his police department that worked in situations where they needed this special type of help.

He eventually found Joe as his partner and they have helped hundreds of people get the help they need.

Because of how well Ernie and Joe's work has helped the community, all police academies in San Antonio are now required to take a lot more of these classes. Now, Ernie and Joe help teach the class that inspired Ernie all those years ago. "We help teach officers how to treat the individual as a patient and not as a criminal. If we spend a little bit more time with people, talking to them, they are more likely to allow us to give them help."

If you're interested in becoming a police officer, taking an improv class might not seem related, however, thinking on your feet is one of the most important skills that a police officer can have. Listening and fast thinking are the key reasons that Ernie and Joe have been able to help so many people. If you can learn now how to think quickly, while still making smart and safe decisions, you are going to make a great police officer.

Dream of Helping to Fight Fires

LIKE

Harriet Duren and Chief Rochelle Jones

Do you have friends that you are so close to that they feel like family? This is how most firefighters would describe being a part of a fire department. Because you never know when you will be called for a fire, firefighters gather at the fire station waiting for the alarm to ring. They even have family meals together and everyone takes turns cooking. Two important family members of the New York Fire Department are firefighter Harriet Duren and Chief "Rocky" Jones.

Harriet Duren was a schoolteacher and frustrated by seeing men who were making more money than her for doing the same job. *So,* she thought to herself, *I need to find a job where men and women were required to be paid equal.* It turns out that being a firefighter is one of those jobs. She trained for a whole year, six days a week to gain the strength it took to pass the difficult, physical test that is required to become a firefighter in New York City. Once she got the idea in her head, she says, "I really wanted to make history in New York City."

Rochelle (or Rocky as her fellow firefighters call her) was the daughter of a firefighter. Although her father was nervous about her being the first female to join the New York City Fire Department, he decided that if a woman was going to break the barrier, it might as well be his daughter.

Rocky thinks back on her first fire and says, "My first job, my knees were actually knocking. The call comes in and the alarm goes off. The adrenaline starts right then and there."

Rocky jokes that she knew very little about firefighting before she started her training. It was during training that she learned that there are trucks and engines and they are treated as two different groups. Trucks contain the tools and the ladders. They do search, entry and get the air moving. Engines control the water and the hose.

Harriet thinks that, "the engine is the most important part, because we have the water and without the water, you can't put the fire out!"

Both women struggled a bit when they were new because it was hard to be the only women. However, as firefighters are known for, over time, they accepted them as part of their families. Rocky even went on to be the first female fire chief of the New York City Fire Department.

Both women also lived through the tragedy of September 11th where hundreds of firefighters sacrificed their lives to help save people. Being a firefighter isn't only about having the skill and strength, but also about what's in your heart. It's about being brave and putting the safety of others before your own. That's a very big thing to do whether you're a man or a woman.

If you're thinking about becoming a firefighter, something you can do today to be ready is to play a team sport. Not only will it help you to build the physical strength required for the test and the job, but it will also teach you the very important lessons of teamwork. Firefighters work as a large group on both the truck and the engine and have to be able to work quickly and make split second decisions together. Team sports can help teach you this.

Dream of helping a Good Cause

LIKE

T. Morgan Dixon and Vanessa Garrison

If you could help prevent someone you know from getting sick, would you? Of course you would. That is how T. Morgan Dixon and Vanessa Garrison felt when they realized women, especially Black women, have such a high risk of heart disease. In fact, it's the number one reason that grandmothers, mothers, and aunts pass away every year. The worst part is that it's preventable. T. Morgan and Vanessa started a nonprofit to help stop this disease. Nonprofits are special because they work for a good cause and the money made goes into making the world better.

Vanessa came to this realization as a young teenager. Her grandmother had eleven children and many grandchildren. She helped to cook and care for all of them and as a result maybe did not care for her own self as much as she should have. One night after she helped Vanessa with her hair, she went to bed and her heart failed in her sleep. Her grandmother was only sixty five years old. She looked around her family and saw that this same thing was happening to others that she loved and knew she had to do something to help her loved ones take care of their health and bring attention to the specific group of women this disease was hurting.

Morgan was teaching school and learned Black women have a better chance of getting heart disease than white women and that some form of this disease would likely impact half of the girls in her class. She wanted to take some action. She took girls from her class out on hikes and taught them the importance of walking. She learned that walking just 30 minutes a day could decrease the risk of lots of illnesses, including heart disease. She taught them that walking is the single most powerful thing that a woman can do for her health.

So, Morgan and Vanessa, who met and became friends in college, got together and combined their shared beliefs in "radical self care." They called on women to walk with them, not just to heal their bodies, but to inspire others and reclaim the streets of their neighborhoods.

Morgan says, "We knew we were on to something, because from Harriet Tubman to the women in Montgomery, when Black women walk, things change."

Vanessa says, "We are not a workout group. We are an army of women who are sick and tired of being sick and tired."

The walking was working and people were taking notice. They started getting big donations and awards. Michelle Obama even Tweeted about them! Most importantly, people were taking action. They turned their idea into a nonprofit called GirlTrek. This made their cause official and they could run it like a business.

Vanessa tells a story about a woman named Susie in Philadelphia, who walked past an abandoned building in her neighborhood every day. She decided, "I'm not waiting. Let me rally my team. Let me grab some supplies. Let me do what no one else has done for me and my community and fix this building."

If you like the idea of going to work for a company that is 100% dedicated to a good cause, like a nonprofit, this doesn't mean that you work for free. It means that you rely on the good will of donations, government grants, or company sponsorships. A great way to learn about this is to find a non-profit near you and get involved. Your place of worship, local YMCA, or community board is a great place to find these organizations.

Dream of Helping People Get Clean Water

LIKE

Joe Madiath

When you go to your sink and turn it on, where does the water come from? When you run the bath water, is it clean enough to bathe in? When you flush the toilet, where does it all go?

One of the most basic needs we have as humans is clean water and if you have it, you likely don't realize that someone is responsible for making sure that the dirty water leaves your house and that clean water comes into your home. These people work in public health and policy.

For others that don't have it, it's a big problem and one of the biggest reasons that people in their countries get sick and can't get better. Joe Madiath says, "It is very fashionable and proper to speak about food in all its forms, all its colors, aromas and tastes. But after the food goes through the digestive system, when it is thrown out, it is no longer fashionable to speak about it. It is rather revolting."

When Joe was a child in India, he showed signs of his love for the well being of others. He organized young workers to fight for better working conditions; the problem was that the person employing these people was his own father!

As he got older, Joe set off to see more of India. Town after town, he saw people getting sick because of dirty water. He saw women who were forced to spend all day walking to fetch clean water. He saw children who were not allowed to go to school because they had to help carry this water home. He saw people with horrible stomachaches that could not be cured. He saw people using the bathroom right out in the open without any privacy. He thought, "What is being done isn't enough. Just because people are poor does not mean that this is what they deserve."

Joe, once again, rallied people together and founded Gram Vikas, which translates to "village development" and focuses on water and sanitation for poor communities in India. His idea is that these small villages can work together to get the materials and skills needed to build clean water systems. Each person would have a job and there would be people elected to be in charge and to keep the system going after it was created.

One team would get up in the mornings with a list of all the things they needed to build the water storage tower, the bathrooms, and the plumbing. Everything they need can be purchased locally and sometimes, the government will help them. Once the team secures all the materials, a team is taught how to build the structures they need. What is wonderful is that after the system for their village is done, they now have a skill that they can apply to other types of work and seek better jobs than they had before.

One by one, village by village, Joe and his team have helped 72,000 people to get clean running water into their homes and do it themselves. In those villages, almost no one is getting sick anymore, people have learned new skills, the women don't have to use their whole days carrying water, and children can go to school.

Joe says, "For India and other developing countries, software and spaceships might not be as important as taps and toilets!"

In countries where clean water is more common, there are still lots of jobs that are required to help keep the water clean, from the plumbers that come into your home to the people in charge of the water systems. In countries where clean water isn't as common, there are lots of people needed to solve the problem. We have enough water on earth, but not enough systems to get it where it is needed. This is becoming so important that really good colleges are offering public health and public policy degrees along with business degrees in hopes of creating more minds like Joe's!

Dream of Helping People Travel

LIKE

Beverly Bass

When you ride your bike with the wind in your face, do you enjoy the feeling of freedom it gives you? This is what attracts many people to the transportation industry. Whether you drive a truck on the open road, a train across the country, or fly a plane through the skies, there's a feeling of freedom on the roads and skies as you help move people or cargo from one place to another. Beverly Bass learned about that freedom as a young child and never looked back.

As a little girl, Beverly loved the idea of flight. She would jump off the top of her family's washing machine. As she would fly through the air, she would flap her arms, imagine herself soaring and then quickly drop to the ground without any fear of being hurt. She wasn't afraid as she loved the feeling of flight. One of her favorite activities was to drive to the airport at night. Her and her aunt would watch the airplanes take off and land. She was fascinated with the idea of flying her own plane, but her parents didn't think that it was something she was serious about.

When Beverly turned 19, she decided that she was sick of asking permission and she just did it. She drove out to airport and signed herself up for flying lessons. Her first lesson was as magical as she dreamed it could be. She felt so big in the air and the world down below, so small. That one lesson was all it took. She got home that night and told her parents that she was going to be a pilot.

She continued taking lessons and eventually was able to fly the plane herself, but she still longed to fly a plane with people in it. The problem was that, at that time, men didn't believe that women should be allowed to fly planes. Can you imagine?

Beverly took the jobs that men didn't want. She even flew dead bodies just for the chance to make money flying. Job after job, she proved that flying a plane wasn't about being big and strong it was about being smart and collected.

Finally, the call came. The one she had been waiting for her whole life. American Airlines wanted to hire her as a flight engineer. Her job would be to make sure that all of the systems in the aircraft are working properly. She took the job and kept her eye on the pilot seat only a few feet away. It took two years, but then she did move seats to become co-pilot. A few years later, her seat changed again, this time to captain. At only the age of 34, she was the first female captain at American Airlines. During her first flight as captain, she flew into her hometown and was greeted by hundreds of people who were there to cheer her on and reporters to tell her story.

The male pilots may not have wanted her there at first, but she held her head high and over time would prove herself as a smart and collected captain. Beverly proved her ability to stay calm and collected many years later. She was flying a large plane from Europe the day of September 11th. She was forced to land her plane in a small town in Canada with 37 other planes that were not expected to land there that day. The people of the town all came together to feed, house, and clothe over 7,000 people that landed in their town of only 9,400 people. The story of that day was made into a hit Broadway musical and the song "Me and the Sky" tells the story of Beverly's journey.

"Never let anyone tell you that you can't. Can't is the worst word in the English language. Believe in yourself and know that you can do anything you set your mind to," says Beverly.

A lot of museums contain life-sized trucks, tractors, trains or airplanes where you can sit in the captain's chair and experience what it really feels like to be in a transportation vehicle of such great size. If you're a female thinking about becoming a pilot, Beverly has a scholarship program that is funded by an organization that she started called The International Society of Women Airline Pilots.

Dream of Helping Fix Smiles

LIKE

Dr. Bill Magee

When you're happy, how do you express this to others? You smile! Imagine if you were unable to smile or were too ashamed to smile and share your good feelings with others. People in the dental profession help us keep our smiles healthy. Therefore, we can share our happiness with the world. Dr. Bill Magee studied dentistry and surgery. He used his skills to help people in countries without good health care to repair cleft lips and restore their smiles. A cleft lip or a cleft palate is when the lip or roof of the mouth does not form properly while a baby is developing before birth. This makes speaking or eating difficult, but it can be corrected with a surgery.

It all started with an act of kindness.

Dr. Magee and his wife traveled to the Philippines to volunteer. They believed that, when you are given much in your life, you should take the time to give back. However, when they arrived, they found that there were hundreds of children and adults that needed their help. As much as they wanted to, they could only help a small portion of the people who needed this surgery. This broke their hearts. They promised themselves that one day they would return with the means to help more people.

They went home and found more doctors, more money and more equipment. Then, they returned to the Philippines. They were able to help more people, but still they didn't feel as if they could help enough.

Every three minutes, a baby with a cleft lip is born. So, they knew they needed a lot more help. Thus, they started a larger company called "Operation Smile." It recruits more doctors, more money, and more equipment than they could provide on their own. With "Operation Smile," Dr. Magee and his wife organize missions to over thirty countries.

Dr. Magee met a man on one of his missions. He'd gone thirty-five years with a cleft lip, and Dr. Magee was able to help him. That very same day, he brought him back to his mother. She thought there was a mistake because she didn't recognize her own son. The doctor told him that, " I used my gifts to fix your lip. Now, you must use what gifts you have to pay it forward and help others."

If you're not quite sure about being a doctor but love the idea of improving people's smiles, you can also be a dental hygienist. These are the people that help clean teeth and assist the doctor with his work.

If you're interested in dentistry and helping people to have beautiful smiles, you can get involved with "Operation Smile" when you're in high school. Dr. Bill Magee and his wife started with their own kids as volunteers, and realized what great assistants they made. They teach primary health care. They teach people how to care for their teeth and eat right. A similar organization,

"Smile Train," also works with students that start in high school. You might be a bit young today, but you can start researching what you need to do to get involved and where you might want to travel as a volunteer!

Dream of Helping Improve Sight

LIKE

Dr. Andrew Bastawrous

Have you had to visit an eye doctor yet? What did the doctor have you do? Most likely, you had to read a chart on the wall so the doctor could measure how far you can see. You might've had to look into a big machine where they could make sure your eye is healthy. Our eyes are so important that we need special doctors who understand every aspect of our eyes, how they change and how to best preserve our sight.

Not everyone in the world has access to an eye doctor. This means that some people are blind simply because there are no eye doctors.

When Dr. Andrew Bastawrous learned how many people couldn't see because of a lack of doctors, he knew he had to do something. He packed up his family and moved to Africa where he thought he could help.

When they arrived and started working, the lights went out!

They flew over all their big testing equipment, but none of it would work if they didn't have electricity. Dr. Andrew Bastawrous thought and thought about what to do. As he looked around, he realized, everyone was holding a phone. "That's it," he thought, "A phone has a camera. Why can't we use that to take pictures of the eye? You can play games on your phone, so why couldn't you take an eye test on your phone?"

Dr. Bastawrous invented something that anyone can connect to his or her phone. It would take a picture of the inside of your eye. Imagine that - taking a picture of the inside of your eye using your phone.

One woman, who had already gone blind, was not able to see any of her grandchildren being born. After years and years of waiting, all she had to do was send a text. She didn't have to leave her house because someone could come to her. It was easy for doctors to travel since there was no heavy equipment to carry. The doctor arrived on his bike, took out his phone and knew how to help her. "You will see again," he said. He was able to restore her sight and she could see the grandchildren for the first time.

"We used to have the cures, but no way to deliver them to everyone who needed it. Now, with just our phones, we can travel anywhere that a phone can go, which is just about anywhere!"

You can take care of your eyes today so that you have healthy eyes your whole life. Carrots and oranges are not only a great snack, but they have nutrients that are good for your eyes.

Take frequent breaks from your devices, as staring at a screen for too long is not good for your sight.

Finally, your eyes can get harmed from the sun, just like your skin can. Be sure when you are outside on a sunny day to wear a hat or sunglasses. Take good care of your eyes, because who knows? Maybe one day you will be able to help give someone the gift of sight, just like Dr. Andrew Bastawrous.

By Holly A. Sharp

Dream of Helping Animals

LIKE

Dr. Pol

Animals get sick, just like us. They need regular checkups and care when they are unwell. It might be your family dog or cat, a whale at Sea World, a penguin at the zoo or a cow on a farm. Dr. Pol is a veterinarian that cares for large animals like cows and horses. He loves all animals big and small and has cared for them his entire life.

Dr. Pol was born on a dairy farm in the Netherlands. He was the only one of the children in the family who woke up early to help his father with the animals. At one year old, he was caring for a chicken that could not lay eggs. By the time he was twelve, he was trusted to help a pig give birth. Assisting the mother pig to deliver her baby was so satisfying. At that point, he knew then that he wanted to be a veterinarian.

Dr. Pol moved to Michigan to marry his wife, whom he met through an exchange program. He studied the different cities and discovered that there was an area that had a lot of farm animals. Though, it had few veterinarians. Before he even had his equipment ordered, his phone was already ringing. A farmer had a cow giving birth and needed his help.

He has delivered hundreds of calves, but one particular birth brought tears to his eyes.

He arrived at the farm and the farmer was worried that the calf being born wasn't breathing. He helped the cow give birth to the calf but his fears were true. The calf wasn't breathing. He performed different movements to help start the breathing including pouring water over its head. Just when everyone thought that nothing else could be done, the calf took a breath. It was moments like this that made all of the middle-of-dinner and late-night calls worth it.

His son was working in California on TV and movies and had a thought: "My Dad is such a character and his job would be interesting to kids. So, I should film him for a TV show!" Thus, he moved back home to Michigan and followed him around for a week with a camera.

He filmed everything from small animals in his daily veterinary practice to the large animals he saw on the farm. National Geographic loved the idea, and so, the show has been on television for seventeen seasons.

If you're interested in becoming a veterinarian, Dr. Pol's show (called *The Incredible Dr. Pol*) is a great place to learn about what it's truly like to care for animals.

As Dr. Pol would say, "You have to let the animal tell you what is wrong with it." Animals can't speak, so you have to be skilled at looking at looking for clues and symptoms to treat an animal in distress properly. You may love animals, but after watching the show, you'll know if you love all the other things that come along with caring for them when they are sick!

Dream of Helping People Walk

LIKE

Professor Hugh Herr

Have you ever tried to catch a salamander? You reach your hands down, scoop it up and open your hand. Except, you only find a tail and nothing else. This animal has the ability to lose its leg or tail and grow a new one! Unfortunately, this is not true for humans. Some people are born without arms or legs and others have had an accident. Medical engineers like Hugh Herr specialize in building body parts. In fact, he also wears the legs that he designed.

Hugh Herr was in an accident that caused him to lose the lower parts of his legs. He says that he has bionic powers. He can think about moving his legs and his brain will send signals to his muscles. Small computers in his bionic limbs decode these brain signals, moving his legs the way he wanted.

His goal is to move from being bionic to being a cyborg.

To have cyborg abilities, he would be able to feel his artificial legs. Him and his team are creating a process where a surgeon would connect the new legs to certain muscles. As a result, the computers inside the leg would help the brain to feel the movement.

Professor Herr was able to help a man who was an avid rock climber. He would climb to great heights and it was the greatest joy of his life. After he had an accident, he didn't think he would ever climb again.

Professor Herr put together what he called "Team Cyborg."

This was a team of surgeons, scientists and engineers that would work together to connect his ankle muscle to his new leg. This surgery would recreate the link between his ankle and his brain. Now, he is a rock-climbing cyborg! He has normal ankle-foot feelings, even with a blindfold on. He said, "The robot is now a part of me. I don't feel like a cyborg. I just feel like I have my leg back."

Professor Herr believes that, with this technology, we will see people become superheroes.

"We will jump higher and run faster than ever before."

You can learn more about the technology that Professor Herr and his team are developing. The Center for Extreme Bionics at MIT has a list of all the projects that him and his team are working on.

You can also prepare for a career in this field by learning as much as you can about both the human body and robotics.

As you will likely see in this book, learning about robotics can open up many different types of opportunities. A simple search on YouTube can provide ideas for robots you can make at home. There are also kits available that contain all the parts you need to learn about making a robot come to life.

Dream of Helping People With "Mind Health"

LIKE

Andy Puddicombe

When your arm hurts, you go and see a doctor. When your head hurts, you take medicine. But is it possible for your mind to hurt? Andy Puddicombe would say, "Yes it is." He says that, "The mind is our most valuable and precious resource, through which we experience every single moment of our life. And yet, we don't take any time out to look after it. In fact, we spend more time looking after our cars, our clothes and our hair."

Growing up, Andy's Puddicombe's grandparents and parents believed in the power of meditation and would practice it often. Meditation is the practice of trying to calm your mind.

When he was eleven years old, he went to his first meditation class. He was more excited that it might be like what he saw in Kung Fu movies. Secretly, he hoped that maybe he would learn to fly in one of these classes. Unfortunately for young Andy Puddicombe, this did not happen.

It did, however, give him a tool he could use when he was in college. It was there that he faced a lot of stress and personal loss. He was having a difficult time coping and his mind was filled with lots of difficult emotions. Every time he got rid of one, a new one seemed to pop up.

Andy Puddicombe remembered back to the calming meditation classes of his childhood, but he wanted to do more than meditate. He wanted to know everything there was to know about caring for your mind through meditation. He left his home in England and went to India to be a monk.

Being a monk meant giving up most of the things he owned, living with other men who have done the same, and learning to calm your mind while living in the service of others. The dedication to calming your mind was so serious that even his itching was part of his practice. He describes the act of not itching as a discomfort you should learn to control. He says that, "Often when we have a discomfort in our lives, we are quick to react to it. Give it your attention and think about it, but I learned to be okay with the discomfort. Not scratching helps teach our mind to not react immediately to something."

He benefited so much from his years of study and wanted to help others learn to cope with hard emotions. Still, he realized that, "Everyone didn't necessarily relate to a bald-headed monk in a skirt smelling like incense. There must be a better way to present this practice."

He met with a good friend and this friend told him to make an app. So, he did. Now this app (Headspace), which teaches meditation through ten-minute sessions, has been downloaded by millions of people and has helped improve the "mind health" of so many.

Helping people to have better "mind health" can come in many forms. Andy Puddicombe's approach is through meditation. However, there are also doctors and therapists that help you to talk about the things that are bothering you and work through how to feel better about them.

There are "mind health" doctors for kids and for adults. It is okay to feel sad or scared about something. Sometimes it is easier to talk to someone who knows how to help. If you ever feel sadder than you can manage, scared or unsure of whom you can talk to, ask a teacher for help and they can find the right person for you to talk to.

Mind health matters just as much as body health.

Dream of Helping People Get Medication

LIKE

The SIRUM Team

What happens when you don't feel well? You go to the doctor and sometimes the doctor gives you medication to take. In order to get your medication, you have to go to a place called a pharmacy. There, a person who is specially trained in understanding lots of different types of medication will give you pills or syrup to take. One of the ways you can work with medication is to be one of these specially trained people. They are called pharmacists. Another way is to help improve the system of how people get their medication.

A group of college students formed a company called SIRUM, where they are helping people get medication by developing a "medicine recycling program."

It all started with an island in South East Asia.

The island was hit by a wave, but not just any wave. A wave so large that it knocked down all the buildings, all the homes and many of the hospitals. Many people were sick and needed medication. Adam Kircher decided to volunteer his time and go to the island to help the people find the supplies they needed. What he found was that this was a hard job. There were supplies, like medication, and there were people who needed that medication, although, there was not a good system for people to find them.

Next came Kiah Williams.

She came from a family that understood poverty and her parents were pushing her to be the first doctor in the family. To get closer to medicine, she would work at health care clinics and community centers and was surprised by how many people she saw who could not afford to buy their medication. Many had to choose between medicine, food or rent. In the United States, medicine is not the same price for everyone. In fact, often the poorest have to pay more.

Adam Kircher and Kiah Williams found each other when they both decided to return to school. Both realized getting medication wasn't a small issue. Ten million Americans can't afford the medications that they should be taking. They studied the problem and realized the two issues they saw could be solved using waste! Well, not really waste, but left-over medication that was going to simply be thrown away.

There are ten billion dollars' worth of safe, perfectly good medication that gets thrown away every year. Some of the extra medication comes from companies that make extra amounts, but it never get sold. It also comes from hospitals that get the medication, but for lots of reasons, the patient never takes it.

Adam, Kiah and third team member Georoge figured out how to collect the extra medication that no one was using and get it to the people who couldn't afford their medication. Kiah William says, "No one should ever be sick and not be able to get the medication that makes them better. If we can recycle a can, why can't we recycle medication? It doesn't have to be easy, only possible."

The next time you are in a store with a pharmacy, ask your parents if you can stop by and meet them. They love their patients and they would be happy to spend a few minutes talking to you and showing you what they do!

Dream of Helping During Emergencies

LIKE

Kevin Hazzard

Paramedics are the people that arrive in an ambulance when someone is hurt and calls 9-1-1. Kevin Hazzard says that, "I didn't grow up wanting to be an EMT (emergency medical technician), nor did I know If I would like it. What I did know is that I wanted to get hip-deep in the things that matter. I want to know if I could be counted on."

After September 11th,, many people stepped up to help with the recovery in New York City. During this time, Kevin Hazzard felt that something was missing from his life. He wanted to test himself. He wanted to see how he might respond to future pressure and danger if he needed to be the one to step up. So, he signed up for emergency medical training.

Kevin knew nothing about medicine, only that he wanted to test his ability to respond to danger. The teacher stood in front of the class, explaining that emergency work was a very personal type of medicine. "It's not like being a doctor where you can run tests or get access to records. Instead, you have to act in the moment. Patients don't come to us; we go to them. Where and how we find them is part of the story. Once in the field, we don't have tests or results to help us figure out what is wrong. We have a blood pressure cuff, a stethoscope, a wristwatch and a flashlight," said the teacher.

Eight months later, Kevin Hazzard was driving an ambulance and saving lives. Some doctors take almost eight years before they are working on their own!

One of the first calls that Kevin took as a new paramedic was on Thanksgiving. A family was enjoying dinner with their grandmother, who was eating and talking, and all of a sudden choked on her food. Unable to breathe, no one knew what to do. The family called 9-1-1 and Kevin helped remove the food from her throat, helping her breathe again.

For many people, medical emergencies are very scary. Often they don't know how to help. As a paramedic, you come into someone's home during this scary time and save them. Each patient is different because you're out in the "real world." With different situations, your reaction is different every time.

In the ten years that Kevin Hazzard worked as a paramedic, he saw many different types of emergencies, including a woman at an aquarium who was stung by a stingray. Looking back at the thousands of people he put in his ambulance.

Kevin Hazzard says, "You don't have to be heroic, but you do have to enjoy the chaos. The normal reaction when someone faces an emergency is to run away or call someone else to help. You have to be the one that wants to run in and do what it takes."

If you think that you have what it takes to be a paramedic, you should start by taking basic life-saving classes like the CPR that Kevin had to perform on the choking grandmother. These classes have full-sized dummies to practice on as you learn. It gives you an idea of what can happen in an actual emergency. You might save someone's life.

Dream of Developing Medical Inventions

LIKE

Anushka Naiknaware

You don't have to go to medical school to work in the medical field. There are a lot of ways that you can help improve people's health. One of those ways is to help develop the things that doctors and nurses use as they work to make you feel better.

This can be something as simple as a bandage.

Once upon a time, kids would fall and scrape their knees. But, there weren't Band-Aids to cover their scrapes. Someone had to invent the idea of a bandage sticking to your skin. It's such a simple idea with so much value. When Anushka Naiknaware was only thirteen years old, she learned something about bandages that startled her. Bandages can actually make people sick.

She did some more reading and learned that a chronic wound is when someone gets a normal cut. Though in this case, it doesn't heal properly. The problem is the bandage. It happens a lot and it happens to a lot of people.

Think about when you get a scab. If you change your bandage too often, it can pull the scab off or start bleeding again. However, if you don't change it often enough, it doesn't get enough air and it won't heal.

Naiknaware thought that this was a straightforward problem. She needed to make a bandage that could alert doctors when it was the right time to change it. This meant measuring how much air and water was inside the bandage.

Her parents fully supported her efforts to experiment with science and let her turn their garage into her lab.

She started working on this problem and like any good scientist, she started experimenting. She had to use her own money to buy all of her supplies; however, as her idea got better and better, she was winning science fairs and using that money to pay for better materials.

Her final bandage had tiny monitors inside that would alert the caregiver that it was dried out just enough to be changed. She started sharing her idea with people and they agreed it was a good idea. So, she entered her idea into a Google Science Fair.

She became the youngest person to ever win this award!

Anushka Naiknaware says, "Even though I'm a fourteen-year-old, working in her garage on something that she doesn't completely understand, I can still make a difference and contribute to the field. And that's what inspired me to keep going. I hope it inspires many others to also do work like this, even though they're not very sure about it."

You may not have an idea today on how to improve the medical community, but science fairs are a great place to get inspired. Find online or in-person fairs and look at what problems people are trying to solve. Maybe you'll think of your own way to solve a problem that someone has pointed out. Then, start experimenting.

You may fail ninety-nine times, but who knows what might happen if you make something new on the hundredth try?

Dream of Helping
Your Family

LIKE

Kristina Kuzmic

There are so many things that you need to learn before you are a grown up. There are lots of people in your life that will help teach you what you need to know, but no one is more important than the person raising you.

This might be a mom, a dad, a grandparent, or a guardian. For some families, they make the choice to dedicate someone to be the fulltime teacher at home. Raising your future children fulltime is a wonderful gift and can be for a short time or for their whole lives. Kristina Kuzmic is a mom who loves raising her kids and gives advice to other moms (usually with jokes).

Kristina always wanted a family, a big one.

She started babysitting as a teenager and would make observations about the type of mom that she wanted to be. One girl that she was babysitting was only five years old, but she would sit and color for hours. Kristina asked the girl if she wanted to be an artist when she grew up. The girl looked at her in confusion and said, "But I am already an artist." Kristina realized that kids are not adults in training. They're real people just like us. She was excited to have her own to see who they would become.

Years later, when Kristina had her own baby, she was having lots of emotions about being a new mom. She had experience making videos at home, so she decided that she would make videos about being a mom.

She used a lot of jokes in her videos. She says, "I find humor in every nook and cranny of motherhood while shoving brownies in my mouth and drinking coffee straight out of the pot.

I love humor, I need humor. Without it, it's like eating soup with a fork. You'll get a tiny amount of nourishment, but you miss out on so much goodness." A celebrity found one of her videos and it was spread all over the Internet. Now thousands of moms watch her videos to listen to her advice and jokes.

One of the things that she talks about is how to help her kids be themselves. One of her kids has a very big personality and likes to talk a lot. When they have company over, she prepares a list of questions for him to ask their guests so that his energy is put to good use.

Another thing she believes is that families should support each other's dreams. When they blow out their birthday candles, they say their wishes out loud so that they can celebrate them and make them come true together.

When she gives her kids advice about what types of careers they might have, she says you should figure out two things. First, what things do you like: math, art, science, reading—whatever. Second, what about the world makes you mad? What do you want to change? If you're good at drawing and are frustrated by world hunger, what can you draw to change the way that people think or act?

If you think that you might want to be a parent, do what Kristina did. Take babysitting jobs when you're old enough or help with siblings or cousins. Take note of the different ages of kids you help with and how they are different at each age.

Dream of helping a Team

LIKE

Coach Dru Joyce II

Many of the sports teams that you may play on are led by volunteers, however, there are teams in high school, college, and in professional sports that require skilled coaches to lead them. This is true of every sport for both boys and girls. What makes coaching special is that it isn't just about the sport. It's about being a good leader and motivating people to be their best. If you like sports and are the type of person that likes to encourage and motivate others, maybe you would be a good coach!

Dru Joyce was the coach of one of the most famous and successful high school basketball teams to ever play the game, but he never actually intended to be a basketball coach. His son was interested in playing basketball, but needed to form a team to play in competitions. Both father and son set out to find other kids to be on their team. The next member was LeBron James. Dru noticed him playing at a local recreation center and saw something special in him. Over the next few years they added Schea Cotton, Willie McGee, and Romeo Travis to the team. This earned them the nickname "the Fab 5."

When the boys first got together under Coach Dru, they were only in 5th grade playing on a tiny court, 20 feet shorter than regulation with weird flooring. It was like bouncing a ball on your kitchen floor! This didn't stop Coach Dru or his team. He knew that these boys could be something special. He also knew that given the right conditions these boys, who came from challenging backgrounds, could have their lives changed by basketball.

For seven years, Coach Dru stayed with the boys every step of the way. Then, suddenly in 11th grade, the boys found themselves without a coach. Coach Dru wanted the job, but worried that he didn't have enough experience to take over. They had already won two state championships. What if they lost their shot at a third one? Everyone would think it was his fault. The boys were gaining celebrity status, playing in front of thousands of people and giving out autographs. Despite his fears, he took the job. Coach Dru wanted so badly for the boys to have a chance at continuing to win. He said, "I never intended to be a coach. I was just helping out my son. I read as many books and watched as many videos as I could."

Then came their 1st state championship under coach Dru, and they lost. This is when Coach Dru realized that coaching was about being a coach. "I took a step back and realized that this was not about winning or losing, but about turning these boys into men." He got them all in a circle holding shoulders and said, "This is what this team is going to be about now: self confidence, teamwork and respect. If you need to leave, I will understand."

The next year, with new focus, his team made it all the way to the national championship— the biggest game you can play. He told the team to play from their heart for the last time together. Coach Dru and his son hugged on the court with tears in their eyes celebrating the team's victory.

Coach Dru may not have been an expert in basketball, but he understood what it took to be a good leader, a good father, and a good mentor. Because of this, they were a great team. According to LeBron James, "We were winning because we respected Coach Dru as a coach, as a mentor, and as a leader."

While Coach Dru found coaching through his son, many successful coaches prepare to become coaches by studying physical education and leadership, often having played the sport themselves. There are tons of documentaries about great athletes and sports teams featuring the coaches that got them there. If you're on a team at school, observe how your coach motivates you and others to play your best.

Dream of Helping to Motivate People

LIKE

Tony Robbins

When you're standing at the pitching mound, focused on the baseball coming at you and deciding whether or not to swing, all eyes are on you. The ball comes in low and you decide to let it fly by. "Good Eye!" someone yells from the sidelines. It feels good to have someone rooting for you. This is what motivational speakers or personal coaches do. They help people feel good about themselves. Confidence and happiness don't always come easy and motivational speakers like Tony Robbins encourage others to live their best lives.

Tony had a difficult childhood, growing up in a household with a lot of uncertainty. He knew that the one thing he wanted as an adult was to make sure that the people around him felt safe, secure, and loved. He had no idea that this desire would make him one of the most successful motivational speakers and coaches of all time.

When Tony was in high school, he was in a speech class. In an attempt to impress a girl that was in the class, he would tell stories to entertain the class. "Tony, please stay after class," the teacher announced one day as the bell rang.

Uh-oh, thought Tony.

"Do you know why I asked you to stay?" asked the teacher. With a guilty look on his face, Tony was about to answer that is was because he was goofing off. "No," the teacher cut him off, "You are here because I want to tell you that you have a special gift. You can captivate a room of kids who don't really care to listen. You are not a speaker—you are a communicator."

He handed Tony a piece of paper with a speech on it called "Free Will." Tony read it and got tears in his eyes. The speech was about never giving up and having the will to keep going. He felt it captured how difficult his home life was. He entered a speech competition and used "Free Will" to move the audience to tears as well. He won first place. He entered other competitions and kept winning. Tony realized that his teacher was right. He had a special gift for reaching people with his words.

Tony spent many years working to be able to give others the advice they needed. Every day he would repeat over and over, "I'm unstoppable. I'm unstoppable. I'm unstoppable." He spent years giving speeches and writing books to help people. Tony is driven to help others, "I have an obsession to help. It makes me feel like my life has deep meaning."

Once per year, Tony gathers thousands of people in a single room for six days. They are together from early morning until late at night. During this time, Tony teaches them lessons about how to be happy. He picks people out of the audience and says, "I'm not here to fix you, and you're not broken. Your life can change in a moment and I want to help you find that moment." He listens to their stories and helps the people understand that they're capable of becoming anything they want. He believes that people shouldn't wait around for life to happen to them. He helps everyone in the room learn from the lessons of the people he chooses. At the end of six days, people leave happier and more excited about their lives.

Tony's advice to anyone who wants to do what he does is to be dedicated to helping others. Of all the tools you have, listening is the most powerful. When a friend is sad, listen to them. Volunteer at a senior home and listen to the stories that the people living there have to tell you. When your sibling is feeling grumpy, instead of brushing them off, ask what is bothering them. Great motivators start as great listeners.

Dream of Helping People Learn

LIKE

Sal Khan

Do you have a younger sibling? Do you enjoy showing them how to do something difficult? Or, maybe you're the younger sibling or cousin and you rely on your older family members to teach you new things. Either way, that is what teaching is about, helping someone to grow. The teachers that you're aware of are probably the ones at your school, but you can teach any age just about any topic. If you wanted to take an art class on the weekends, that requires a teacher. If you want to attend college, those require teachers called professors. You can teach online as well as in the classroom. In the year 2020, many kids have experienced learning through the Internet. Sal Khan is an educator who helped develop online learning courses long before they were a part of "normal" life.

Sal believes that learning is important and when his cousins needed some help in school, he offered to be their tutor. He didn't live close by, so he had to tutor them remotely over the computer. To help make it easy to learn on their own, Sal made YouTube videos that were based on the topics they were studying.

The cousins told him, "We like YouTube Sal more than in-person Sal." Instead of letting this hurt his feelings, Sal asked them a simple question, "Why?" They said it was because they could pause and repeat concepts without feeling embarrassed when they didn't understand something at first.

Sal started making more videos on more topics. Soon, people were finding his videos on YouTube and using them for learning as well. Because Sal cared more about helping people grow than making money, he kept all his videos free. He started getting comments and letters from people around the world. One letter said, "My 12-year-old son has autism and has had a terrible time with math. We have tried everything, viewed everything, and bought everything. We stumbled on your video of decimals and got through it. Then we went on to dreaded fractions. Again, he got it. We cannot believe it. He is so excited." Letters like this made him realize that he had a calling as an educator and how good it felt to be helping people.

Sal kept on making videos on lots of different topics. He now has over 2,000 videos and his own online school called the Khan Academy. Now, all sorts of people from all over the world can get an education for free! A young girl in India, whose family didn't have money to send her to school, was able to learn from her one room home because of these videos.

Teachers also started using these videos in the classroom. Instead of teaching during the day and giving homework at night, teachers would assign videos to watch at home and students would now do homework together in the classroom, making sure that everyone understands what they're learning. Sal says, "This is like learning to ride a bicycle. If after 2 weeks you haven't learned how to stop properly, I don't just give you a bad grade and then make you move on to a harder bike. Our classes make it okay to experiment and fail, but you have to get the concept before you're allowed to move on."

If you're interested in becoming a teacher, it's easy to get started. Find something you enjoy doing and teach it to someone else. Maybe it's helping a younger sibling with their ABC's, teaching a friend how to draw your favorite cartoon, or maybe there is someone in your class that you notice is having difficulty with a subject you understand well. Think about how to make your tutoring interesting and remember to be patient with the person learning.

Dream of Helping People Read

LIKE

Dawn Wacek

Reading a book is a special experience. Curling up in your favorite chair or laying in bed at night, your mind is transported to different worlds. You have the ability to learn about endless topics (like what you might be when you grow up!) It also helps you out in the world as well. The more you can read, the more you can do.

Libraries help us make sure that reading isn't just for people who can afford to buy lots of books. Libraries help make sure that anyone and everyone has access to reading. Dawn Wacek is a librarian who believes that there's more we can do to give people access to reading.

Dawn greets each and every person who enters her library by saying, "Hello friend, welcome to the library!" She wants them to think of her as a friend because she knows what a difference a library can make in someone's life. Information is power and the library is the one place where you can fuel that power—for free! Well…almost free.

This is what makes Dawn a special librarian. She believes that libraries shouldn't have late fees. When you check out a book or movie from the library, there is a date you have to bring it back by so that other people have a chance to borrow it as well. If you don't bring it back on time, then you are charged a fine for each day it's late. Dawn, however, has proof that the people who need the library the most aren't coming to the library because they either already have a late fine or are scared of getting one and can't afford to pay it.

Dawn is trying to spread the word about why this is a big deal. Children who read frequently (like you are right now) hear and see more complicated words (like the word complicated!) This leads certain kids to get ahead in reading and writing regardless of what's taught in schools. She believes that if libraries are really meant to be a free resource to help those that might not have easy access to books, then why scare them off with fines? In her library, there are 10,000 people (you read that correctly) who have stopped using the library because they can't afford the late fines. This impacts lots of people at other libraries too. If people are afraid of fines, they'll stay away from the library.

Dawn says that libraries don't need the money from these fines and that it actually costs money to track people down to remind them to pay. Some libraries are adopting the early "Netflix model" where people can take out books and then can't take out more books until the books you have are returned, no matter how long it takes. Another library removed all fines for just children's books, and the number of people who started coming again doubled!

Dawn loves all her friends that come to the library and doesn't want fines to get in the way of more friends coming. Mistakes happen to everyone. She says, "We get busy. Things get lost. Accidents happen. Juice get spilled. Does this mean that if you can't afford the mistake that you are no longer a friend—no!"

If you love the library as much as Dawn does, spend time with a librarian at your local library. Most librarians do this job because they love children and helping people. You're a friend to the librarian and they can teach you about their job or help you learn about just about any topic that might be of interest to you (there are plenty in this book to choose from).

By Holly A. Sharp

Dream of Helping People Manage Money

LIKE

Dave Ramsey

When you get money in a birthday card, what do you do with it? Do you save it in a piggy bank? In a bank account? Do you run out and spend it right away? As you get older, what you do with your money can make a major difference in the quality of your future life. Not everyone is skilled at saving for things like a new home, college education or retirement. Because of this, there are people who are able to help people manage their money so that they have enough. Dave Ramsey has a radio, TV show and book with the single focus of helping people to be smart with their money.

When Dave was a child, he wanted to get a slushie drink from the local gas station. He approached his father for some money and his father asked him, "Where do you think the money I am giving you comes from?" Dave thought about the answer and said, "I suppose your job." "That's right," said his father. "Now, it's your turn to make the money you want for things like slushies. What skill do you have that could help you to make your own money?" Dave decided that this skill was cutting grass. He went to a printer and had 500 business cards made. He went door to door handing out these cards and, by the end of handing them out, he had twenty-seven yards to mow! As he grew up, he continued to find little businesses that he could start and began to appreciate the power of having his own money.

After graduation, he used this money to help him buy several houses with the plan of selling them. It worked so well that he wanted to buy more. So, he borrowed money from a bank (called a loan). There was a problem with the bank and they asked him to pay all the money back at once. He could not. He had to go through a process that forgave him for the money he owed, called bankruptcy. Declaring yourself bankrupt makes it very hard for banks to trust you again. Dave had to learn about managing money and how to start over.

After losing all his money, Dave slowly recovered. A friend asked him how he did it. And so, he showed him how to make a budget. Look at all the money you have, what the bills you have to pay and how much do you need to pay off money you already owe. Think of the money you get from your birthday cards. You could spend it all at once on one big thing, you could buy a few smaller things, or spend some and save some or save it all. This is a budget, because you're figuring out how to manage your money without overspending. His friend was grateful. Dave thought, "This is something that I could be good at."

He started a class at his church about money management that quickly grew. Before long, he was asked to bring his advice to a local radio station. The phones didn't stop ringing the entire time that he was on the show. Dave was so inspired by how much he could help the person on the other end of the phone line that he offered to work for free to have a radio show of his own. The message of the show was simple, but it worked. Don't buy things you can't afford. If you owe money, pay it back. Create a budget and stick to it. Simple.

His show is special because it gives people hope. "It's crazy what people can pull off when they believe they can. But also, it shows what they can't accomplish when they think they can't. The fuel is the hope," says Dave. He started something called the "debt-free scream." When people owed money and paid it off, they would drive from hundreds of miles away. They drove, sometimes for days, to come to the radio station and tell their story. Then they would yell, "I am debt free!!!!"

An important lesson that everyone should learn when young is how to earn and spend money wisely. Dave Ramsey has a collection of books for young children about money management that can help you understand the concepts that people like Dave make a living teaching others.

24

Dream of Helping the Earth
LIKE
Greta Thunberg

Have you ever been so mad about something that you just wanted to scream at the world? You want to slam your door so hard that it shakes the house! That is how Greta Thunberg feels about climate change; only instead of slamming her door and shaking her house, she shook the world. People who work to spread the word about an issue without any motivation of making money are called advocates or activists. Greta is the perfect example of how people of any age can do this. No one will hire you for this job. You have to hire yourself.

When Greta was 11 years old, her teacher showed the class a video of the impact that climate change is having on our planet. The video showed the polar bears that were running out of food and the extreme weather that was causing flooding and storms. She couldn't believe that this was happening to the world that she was supposed to grow up in. She became very sad. So sad, in fact, that she didn't feel like eating or talking. Greta has a type of autism that causes her to have more focus on certain topics than other people might and as a result, very strong emotions.

She finally asked her parents "This can't be real can it? Surely if this were real that the politicians would be taking care of it."

Her father started researching the concerns that her daughter had and he realized that she was right, there wasn't enough being done. To help get t spirits up, her family started doing things to help lower their own impact on the earth. They stopped eating meat while growing their own vegetables, they used different forms of transportation and they even installed solar panels on their home. Slowly, Greta began to eat and talk again. Once she regained her voice, she decided that she needed to be louder, not quieter. She decided that she would not go back to school until the government made a change. She would sit outside the government offices in protest, instead of attending school.

She said, "If the adults don't care about my future, I don't either." Well, some adults did, her parents and teachers. They tried to convince her to find a different way, but her parents saw how happy it made her to be doing something after being so sad for so long.

Her father said, "It was like striking brought her back to life."

The first day, Greta was all by herself with her sign. She sat in protest by herself on a chilly day. The second day, one person joined her, then the next day a few more. Word got around on social media and a few turned into hundreds and then into thousands. Suddenly it was happening in other places around the world as well. Every Friday, people both young and old from all over would march in protest so that their government could see that the decisions they were making now were impacting a new generation of people and those people were demanding that we "make the world Greta again!"

"Fridays for the Future" was happening in cities all over the world. Thousands of people were leaving their schools in protest. It took less than a year to go from sitting by herself in the cold to motivating millions to stand up for their planet. In 2019 Greta was asked to speak at a very important meeting about climate change. Her words at that meeting have become famous around the world.

"This is all wrong. I shouldn't be up here. I should be back in school on the other side of the ocean. Yet you all come to us young people for hope? *How dare you!* You have stolen my dreams and my childhood with your empty words. And yet I'm one of the lucky ones. People are suffering. People are dying. Entire ecosystems are collapsing. We are at the beginning of a mass extinction. And all you can talk about is money and fairy tales of eternal economic growth. How dare you!"

You are never too young to get involved in something you care about. This doesn't mean you need to skip school like Greta did, but talk to your parents about the issues that concern you. Maybe there is a peaceful protest that you can get involved with. Maybe you can write a letter to your politician. Maybe you can create a video to put on social media. Activism isn't a job that you can go find and apply for. It is just something you have to get up and do.

Dream of Helping Chimpanzees

LIKE

Jane Goodall

The destruction of our planet and the animals that live on it should be the problem of all humans, but the truth is that not everyone has the time or energy to make sure that our planet and its animals are cared for. Conservationists are dedicated to caring for the environment and its animals. Jane Goodall started her career as a zoologist, studying chimpanzees in the wild and living among them. Because of the fame she gained for her work, she was able to bring attention to the issues that the chimpanzee faces in their natural habitat. Jane has dedicated her life to creating programs that help these animals.

When Jane was one, her father gave her a stuffed chimpanzee. Her mother was certain it would frighten her, but the stuffed animal became her favorite toy and started her love for chimps. As she grew, Jane spent hours at the top of her favorite tree, in her own leafy paradise, reading books. It was there she read about Tarzan and would daydream what it would be like to live in Africa with the animals and write her own books about them. Jane jokes that, "Some girls daydream about being married and having a family, I would daydream about working with animals in a far-off place." When Jane graduated, she worked as a waitress and saved every penny she earned to get to Africa and live out her childhood dream.

When she arrived in Africa, she found a man who was looking for someone to study chimpanzees in the wild and she jumped at the chance. She believed that the best way to study an animal is when they know you are there, but they ignore you. She had to get to know them and get them to trust her. She told herself, "I want to be close to them, like Dr. Doolittle. I want to move among them without fear, like Tarzan."

Day after day for five months she would go to visit the chimpanzees. In sun, wind or rain she would climb into the forest through brush and snake-filled grass to watch them. Finally, a lone male chimp allowed her to get close and follow him back to his community. Little by little they would allow her to get closer, until one day they would take bananas straight from her hand. From then on, Jane was a part of their world.

She would stay with the chimps from sunrise to sunset and then come home and type up her notes at night. Jane was able to open a window into this fascinating world of animals. Eventually, she had someone filming her work and she was able to share her experience with the world. This made people fell in love with her and her chimpanzees.

Jane realized that after years of studying these animals that she could do more with her famous name. She could protect the chimpanzees as well as study them. She has dedicated 60 years to working with chimpanzees with over half of that time spent building the Jane Goodall Institute, which brings attention to the threats facing this species.

She claims that when she started her conservation work, she has never spent more than three weeks in the same place, traveling the world educating people about her cause. She also works with local communities where chimpanzees live to improve the laws and practices that put these animals in danger.

Jane Goodall started a group called Roots and Shoots (rootsandshoots.org) if you want to learn more about her work. There are many other organizations that focus on conservation work. Use documentaries or reading to figure out the cause that you care about and find a conservation group that you can support or get involved with. You are never too young to make a difference. Just ask Greta Thunberg!

Dream of Helping Giraffes

LIKE

Anne Dagg

Zoos are a fun place to watch animals up close and personal. They are fun for an afternoon out with your family. They're also intended to help us better understand the animals of the world. The people who work with and study these animals are called zoologists, but you don't have to work at a zoo to be a zoologist! A zoologist simply means that you study animals in order to deepen our understanding of them and how they live in the wild. One such woman is Anne Dagg who loves and studies giraffes.

Anne's love of giraffes began at the very young age of three. Her mother took her to the Brookfield Zoo in Chicago where she stood in the shadow of a giraffe. That giraffe would have seemed as tall as a building to a three-year-old. Like a unicorn, she thought, "they are simply unlike any other animal." She asked her parents for a book about giraffes so that she could learn more, but despite all of their searching, they couldn't find any books.

This burning desire didn't go away as she grew older and when she studied biology in college, she was excited to finally learn about giraffes. However, with each passing year, she couldn't find a class that focused on the topic of giraffes. Anne made up her mind that after graduation she would move to Africa and study this animal that had completely captured her attention as a child.

She had a few challenges in getting there. First, a man she really loved asked her to marry him. Her mother encouraged her to follow her dream first. If it was real love, he would wait for her. Second, she couldn't find a place to stay because she was a woman and most of the giraffe habitats only had housing for men. She eventually found a farmer who let her live with him in exchange for helping him with his business.

She bought an old car and would sit in the extreme African heat watching around 30 giraffes per day. She wrote down everything she saw from what they ate, how often they ate, which animals stuck together, how far they would move in a day, when they slept, and how they interacted with each other. The giraffe was a very trusting animal, allowing her to get close to them. Sometimes she would get so close, she could see their giant eyelashes.

Giraffes had never been observed or written about so closely. Anne was soon published in an important scientific journal and would be seen as a pioneer in the world of giraffes in the wild. Today, people study animals all over the world in zoos and in the wild, using much more sophisticated equipment than a journal.

You can become your own zoologist by learning what we already know about animals today.

The National Geographic website has a wonderful database that contains information about every animal you can think of. Start your own "baseball card" collection of animals by printing a picture of the animal and gluing it to the front of an index card and writing your favorite facts about that animal on the back of the card. Before you know it, you'll be an expert on animals and ready to study them in the wild!

You can also check at your local zoo as they often have camps and volunteer programs for kids to start working with animals at a young age.

Dream of Helping Sharks

LIKE

Ocean Ramsey

Biology can sound like a scary science word, but every time you learn about animals, you're studying biology. The study of living things is what biology is all about. A marine biologist studies the animals that live in the ocean.

You can't be named Ocean and not love that great body of water and all the animals in it!

Ocean grew up surfing and scuba diving. Her desire to study marine life increased with each wave she rode and animal she encountered. Even as a young child, she grew up with a love of sharks and did not fear them the way that most people did. She was eight years old when she saw her first shark. The water was so clear that she could see it swim only a few feet below her and she could not take her eyes off of it. It wasn't scary or aggressive. It was beautiful, graceful, and perfect to her.

She knew exactly what she wanted to study, receiving her first degree in marine biology and her second degree in ethology, the study of animal behavior. Specifically, she wanted to learn about sharks. She wondered why most people thought they were scary when the ones she had encountered were so captivating? During college she was teaching scuba diving class and almost every person she taught was afraid to encounter a shark. She explained to them that seeing a shark would be a rare treat, more memorable than scary. On average, sharks attack only seven people per year usually because they fail to follow directions of how to behave in the ocean. In fact, only 1% of sharks are predators, but television and film have made a rare shark attack seem frequent.

She wished that people could see what she saw. "They have these beautiful blue eyes and as they swim past you, you really get to stare into their soul as there are so many layers to them. There's such a level of awareness and consciousness that becomes extremely apparent when they swim by and they really look you up and down. I remember the first great white shark that swam by me, he slowed down and grazed his pectoral fin on the cage, looked at me and I felt in that moment—this is why I am here."

Since so many people are terrified of sharks, their possible endangerment doesn't concern people. However, sharks are in danger of becoming extinct in our lifetime as humans hunt them for sport and food (including a Chinese dish called shark fin soup). In the ocean, sharks remove dead and diseased things from the waters keeping the environment healthy.

In addition to the research that she has conducted around the world, Ocean lives in Hawaii and goes out every day to swim with sharks and study their behavior around humans. She also runs the only company in the United States that will take you out swimming with sharks without a cage. She hopes that by experiencing a shark up close that people will understand sharks the way she does.

On every dive she does, alone or as part of a class, she continues to gather data to show that sharks are less dangerous than people think. She makes this data available for free hoping the information will combat the fears of sharks caused by a lack of scientific information, experience, and the fear imparted by the media.

If you are interested in studying biology, it's helpful to understand living things at a cellular level. You can get a microscope kit and start looking at all sorts of things under it from your own cells, to plant cells and animal cells. Books at your library can help you understand what you are seeing under the telescope. There are numerous websites that focus on marine life, how to become a marine biologist, and groups that protect all marine life including sharks. As climate change increases, the oceans hold many answers about how to preserve our planet.

Dream of Helping Grow Food

LIKE

John and Molly Chester

Think about all the fruits and vegetables you eat every day. Every apple, orange, corn on the cob, carrot and potato was grown on a farm. We need farmers to provide all the food we eat. You would be a good farmer if you love nature and being outside all day. John and Molly Chester weren't born farmers; they left big city life to be closer to nature and became farmers.

John and Molly lived in Los Angeles, California. John worked as a cameraman for TV and movies. Molly had a food blog that was all about healthy eating and natural foods. They both dreamed of being able to live on a farm and grow all the foods they would eat. They longed to have animals around them and to live in a space bigger than their tiny city apartment.

"We wanted a farm straight out of a children's book," John said. They wanted this so badly, but there was never a good time to quit their jobs and move to a farm.

This all changed with a dog named Todd. John and Molly adopted Todd from another family. They promised him that their home would be his last. The problem was that when they left, he would bark all day long. They tried everything, but they got kicked out of their apartment. They couldn't go to another apartment because he would just bark there too. Todd's need to be in nature made them decide it was finally time to buy a farm.

They bought a run-down farm an hour away from the city, named it Apricot Lane, and got to work bringing it back to life.

When they started planning out their farm, everyone, including other farmers, told them that they were crazy. To make money as a farmer, you need to concentrate on a few crops, and you need to use chemicals to keep the bugs from eating your crops. They didn't want to do either.

They wanted to use their 200 acres to create a "traditional farm" where every plant and animal play a role in helping the fruits and vegetables grow. They planted 75 different fruits in what they called "the fruit bowl." John and Molly let the chickens roam free and sold the eggs they made, but they soon discovered the many problems that come with letting nature control the farm.

First, all the fruit was overrun by thousands of snails. Some trees were so covered, you could barely see its trunk! They tried to pick them off, but there were too many. During this time, it had not rained in a very long time. This meant the pond where their ducks swam did not have fresh water and it was hurting them. "What do you do with 100 ducks?" John wondered. He let them loose in the fruit bowl and it turned out that ducks eat snails! They ate over 90,000 snails and turned them into fertilizer for the trees.

John says, "For every new problem that came up, I would take a step back and think about how another part of the farm can solve it. Observation followed by creativity is our biggest tool."

It's rewarding to eat a food that you grow yourself. If you don't have the space in your yard to start and tend your own garden, you can grow certain foods and herbs in an indoor garden. Plan out your garden and don't forget to think about the rest of nature, just like John and Molly. How will you keep bugs and animals from eating your food? Visit a farm and talk to the owners. Despite the hard work, they rarely feel anything but love for their way of life.

DREAM IT & do it

100 POSSIBILITIES, STORIES, REAL-LIFE ROLE MODELS.

FOR GIRLS AND BOYS

INSPIRING ALL THE THINGS YOU CAN BE

HOLLY A. SHARP

Dream of Discovery

ANY DREAM CAN INVOLVE DISCOVERY, IF YOU'RE COMMITTED TO LEARNING

The careers in this section are the ones you can dream of getting if you love learning new things.

Discoverers are committed to learning new things through researching, exploring, and experimenting.

There is an endless amount of amount of things for you to discover:

Dream of looking for things in space
Dream of looking for things from our past
Dream of looking for things that make us safer
Dream of looking for new technologies
Dream of looking for new ideas

Whatever you dream of finding, go out and do it

Dream of Looking for Dinosaurs

LIKE

Peter Larson

If you love dinosaurs, what would be cooler than going for a hike and finding real dinosaur bones? This is what a paleontologist does. They dig around the world looking for fossils, like bones, to help us learn about the planet as it existed millions of years ago. Archeology is similar, as it involves looking for things from the past, but instead of fossils, they are looking for artifacts that belonged to humans in order to better understand the societies that came before us.

Peter Larson started a company that hunted for fossils and his team was responsible for finding Sue, the dinosaur that lives at the Chicago Field Museum today. When Peter was a child, fossils fascinated him. When he was only 4 years old, he found an animal's tooth at his parents' ranch. That was the beginning of his obsession. He wandered their property for hours searching for interesting fossils and rocks. He set up a museum in their shed and charged his parents five cents to come in and see what he collected. He understood the human fascination with things that were a part of our earth's long history. This fascination continued into college where he studied at a school of mining and technology. While in school, he attended his first gem and mineral show, noticing how different collectors were able to sell their findings to museums and collectors. Then and there, Peter decided to start his own paleontology company.

A few years later, on August 12, 1990, one of the members of Peter's team named Susan was out on a hike while the rest of her team was dealing with a flat tire and she came across something unusual. It looked like the spine of a large animal sticking out of the ground. She ran back to find her team. They came back and couldn't believe their eyes. They had found a real Tyrannosaurus Rex! This is how "Sue" the dinosaur got its name, after the woman who found her.

Peter and his partner began digging with big tools at first, but as they got closer and closer to the bones, they used tiny brushes to be sure that they did not harm anything. The most exciting part of digging out the bones was when they found the skull. As they began brushing away the dirt, one by one, the teeth began to appear. For 65 million years this dinosaur sat underground untouched. It still had its teeth! Once they had pulled all of the bones out of the ground, they realized that they had something special. Before this discovery the other T-Rex discoveries had over half of their bones missing. "Sue" still had 90% of her bones, almost an entire skeleton!

It was Peter's dream to create a museum, just like the one he opened when he was a child, but filled with dinosaur bones. Sue would not end up in his museum because there was disagreement between a lot of people over who should be the owner. In the end, it was sold to The Field Museum in Chicago where scientists and dinosaur lovers can visit anytime. Peter went on to find 13 more Tyrannosaurus Rex's after "Sue" and created his dream museum in Hill City, South Dakota.

Scientists believe that there is still so much about our planet's past that we don't know. It is up to the next generation (that's you) of paleontologists to discover. You can start by going to your library and learning what types of fossils are popular where you live. For example, in Michigan, you can find a really cool fossil called the Petoskey stone. Find out where these types of fossils or rocks can be found and go on your own hunt. Maybe, like Susan, you'll get lucky and find something worth sharing with the world!

Dream of Looking For Ways Into Space

LIKE

Stephanie. D Wilson

Lying on your back outside, staring up at the dark, star-filled sky, you might wonder, "What's out there?" Stephanie D. Wilson had the same thought as a child. Because of astronomers, we grew up learning about the sun, the moon, and all the planets in our solar system. However, it's up to astronauts, like Stephanie, to actually voyage into space to explore and learn more. So far, Stephanie has spent 42 hours in space and she is hoping her next stop is the moon!

Her curiosity about space began with a class assignment. The teacher told the class to, "Go find someone to interview who works in a field that is interesting to you." Stephanie thought about all of the questions she had and knew that space was something she wanted to learn more about. She interviewed an astronomer who helped her understand that studying math, science, and engineering would lead her on a path to explore space.

Stephanie chose to study engineering and her astronomer mentor was right. This path of study led her to the Johnson Space Center, where future NASA astronauts go to learn how to adapt and work in space. Stephanie was one of forty-three people chosen to join the training class where 2,500 people applied! She made a huge effort to stand out. Stephanie believes a trait that makes people stand out is being adaptable.

She says, "Astronauts have to be able to transition well between being leaders and followers and make good decisions quickly in an emergency situation or in a situation where resources are limited."

There were many different things that she had to learn in astronaut training school. First, the class learned what to do if their spacecraft landed in water. She put on her space suit and a parachute and a boat dragged her through the water to simulate what happens when landing.

Then, she had to learn how to manage the feeling of weightlessness. She had to learn to fly a T-38 military plane, nicknamed "the vomit comet" because it goes so high and when it dips down you experience 2G (twice the force of gravity) and then a feeling of weightlessness.

She also had to learn to dress herself and move around a space shuttle under water. The training center has a huge pool with a space shuttle at the bottom. Astronauts train how to move around in water because it is the closest simulation to space. Stephanie jokes that, "It's the only job where you have to have help putting on your pants!" They also train to learn things like how to exercise in space, operate the shuttle, build survival fires, use the ejection seat, and land in trees. They have geological training to learn to dig and identify different rocks and other elements.

Once her training was complete, she was chosen to go into space to visit the International Space Station, which is a research laboratory, owned by 5 different countries, permanently docked in space.

Stephanie says, "It was the best 8.5 minutes of my life!" Now, as part of NASA's Artemis program, she is one of 17 astronauts eligible to become the first woman to step foot on the moon. Her advice to aspiring astronauts hoping to take the same journey is to, "Study hard in math and science. If you don't go into the military first, you have to have a degree in a math or science subject."

A fun way to get started on your own training is to ask your parents for help downloading a space exploration app. Some good examples are apps from NASA or Lego City Explorers (Space). Maybe as a birthday or Christmas present you can ask for the "Astronomer" video game! Don't forget, though, that being an astronaut for real requires practicing your math and science skills!

Dream of Looking for Aliens

LIKE

Sara Seager

You've seen pictures of cartoon aliens in books, watched movies that show monsters from outer space, but has it occurred to you that aliens could be real? There are people, like Sara Seager, who are looking for life on other planets. Sara Seager is a real-life alien hunter!

Sara was 10 years old before she sàw stars for the first time. She lived in a city and the city lights made it impossible to see the night sky. One weekend, her father took her and her siblings camping in a place where the skies were completely dark. The first night, she snuck out of her tent while the rest of her family slept. Sara actually felt her heart stop as she saw the stars for the first time. She was in disbelief that she could have gone this long without noticing them. She thought, "I must have been the first person to see the night sky. I must have been the first person in human history that had braved her way outside and looked up. Otherwise the stars would have been something that people talked about, something that children were shown as soon as we could open our eyes."

Sara went on to become a doctor of astronomy and is now an astrophysicist, a type of physicist, who studies space. In order to hunt for aliens, she first needs to find the planets that those aliens would live on. She looks for exoplanets, which are planets outside of our solar system. The gases on these far away planets will help us learn if there are signs of life on that planet . Since we have oxygen in earth's atmosphere our planet supports life. Her job is to study these planets and select which type of gas are on that planet and if they might support life. She is in search of "the Goldilocks planet" one not too big, not too small, not too hot, and not too cold—just right for life to exist.

Sara has some favorite exoplanets. Kepler 16b is a planet where "your shadow always has company." Because it has more than two stars, you would have two shadows and two sunsets. Kepler 186f is "where the grass is always redder on the other side." This planet orbits a red star so there is a hypothesis that if there were plants, they would have different colors than our plants. Kepler 10b might be considered a "hot planet." It's so hot that its lakes would be made from molten lava.

Sara says that being an astrophysicist is like being an explorer. You have to have the stubbornness to move forward no matter what people think. It's taken many years to convince people that she could be right about possible life on these planets.

Her generation is working to study the gases on large planets, but she believes that a future generation will solve how to measure them on smaller and more distant planets. She hopes that your generation will be remembered for laying the roads to space. Wouldn't it be amazing to be remembered for being the first person to find life on another planet?

The stars near our planet are easy to learn about. There are easy to use telescopes and plenty of books at the library where you can learn about the stars that you can see. There are apps you can point at the sky to help you identify the constellations that form shapes, like the big dipper. Try and find a place where the sky will be totally dark at night just as Sara experienced on her camping trip. Be an explorer of the sky!

Dream of Looking at How Space Works

LIKE

Stephen Hawking

If you put a balloon over the top of an empty water bottle and then dip the bottle into warm water, what happens? The balloon inflates. This happens because the air inside of the water bottle is warm and needs more space, so it expands into the space inside of the balloon. Once upon a time, this could be viewed as magic, but because of the study of physics, we understand how and why stuff moves the way it does. Stephen Hawking studied how these ideas work in space.

Stephen Hawking is one of the most famous physicists in the last 100 years because he helped make the understanding of this complex subject easy for people. Stephens's ability to understand complex topics started when he was a child.

He was raised by parents who enjoyed thinking about all sorts of topics and encouraged debate at the dinner table. Stephen loved it and said, "To outsiders, our household seemed crazy, but to me it was a place where my mind was constantly being challenged. My parents taught me to question everything." This curiosity led Stephen to study physics in college and go on to become a doctor of physics! While he was studying, he discovered that he had ALS, Lou Gehrig's disease, which, over time, made it impossible for him to write or speak on his own. This didn't stop Steven. He enlisted the help of others and special computers to continue to do his moving and writing for him. Some believe that because he had to rely completely on his mind, he could see and think of things that others could not.

Stephen researched many topics, but his most recognized work is focused on black holes. A black hole is an area in space with such a strong force of gravity that it pulls in anything that gets close to it. Not even light can escape its force. Before Stephen's research, people believed that nothing ever came out of a black hole.

As Stephen was researching this topic, he predicted that black holes were different from what was commonly believed. Despite the fact that a black hole sucks in everything around it, some particles actually come back out! This must be a mistake!" he said when he looked at his calculations.

It seemed impossible to him that a force so strong, could release anything back out. Others also thought he was wrong as well, but after other scientists reviewed his work, people began to believe him and celebrate his discovery. Knowing more about black holes is a big step in understanding how space works.

While having these eureka moments were the highlight of Stephen's life, he was not satisfied that only he, and other like-minded scientists, were the only ones to understand and get excited by the things they were learning. Without the use of his hands or voice, he wrote a book called *A Brief History of Time*. This book helped explain, in simple language, the beginning of the universe, its structure, and what might happen in the future. While many thought that no one would care about this topic, his book broke a world record for book sales! "I am so happy that I have been able to get people excited about physics," said Stephen, but he didn't see himself as famous. "The notion of fame is a curious thing to me. In my mind, I am a scientist who has been lucky enough to work on some of the fundamental mysteries of our universe."

More than anything, Stephen would want you to know that, "No matter how difficult life might seem, there is always something you can succeed at." Physics doesn't have to be a scary topic that only geniuses can understand.Likeall science topics, there are many experiments that you can do in order to better understand how the world around you works. If you search online or take out books from the library, you can find experiments to do on your own. You can also ask your parents to help you look for experiment kits that specifically teach about physics.

Dream of being a venom scientist

LIKE

Dr. Mandë Holford

Everything in the world is made up of something called matter. Even air is matter. Matter can be in solid form, like an ice cube, liquid form, like water, or gas form, like steam coming from a pot of boiling water. The people who study these different types of matter are called chemists. Chemists study the matter that exists today and combine them in new ways to make new types of mixtures. Dr. Mandë Holford studies the chemistry of animal venom to try and cure diseases.

Dr. Mandë's love of science started as a child running around in a museum. Every day after school, while her parents worked, she and her siblings would go to the natural history museum near where they grew up. At the museum , she would go on "scientific adventures" and uncover something new about how the world worked.

Her love of chemistry grew from the funniest of places, snails. There is a snail called the cone snail that stole her heart. This snail seems innocent enough, however, there are many fish in the sea that would disagree. This snail is what Dr. Mandë calls, "the assassin of the sea," and their weapon of choice is venom. This slow, small snail is able to kill and eat a moving fish. The snail waits patiently and lures in the fish with a bright, orange, tongue-like appendage. Then the snail zaps the fish with its toxins. The toxins in the venom get in the way of the fish's cells talking to each other and make the fish unable to move. That's some crazy chemistry!

The ability to be bad is also what makes venom good. Dr. Mandë says that venom is, "both a villain and a super hero." It is a villain because it can be used to hurt the blood, brain, or cell activity in a perfectly healthy being; however, it can also attack things that are bad, like cancer.

In her laboratory, Dr. Mandë studies venom of all sorts of sea snails. She is trying to figure out how to make the chemistry of their venom fight cancer. This is possible because cancer tumors are cells. Just like how the snail venom attacked the nerve cells in the fish, causing them to stop communicating, and the fish to stop moving, venom might be able to stop cancer cells from communicating and to stop growing.

Dr. Mandë is studying the chemistry in venom to figure out the right mixture that causes this "communication block" between cancer cells. This is exciting work, but she is actually one of many doctors over the last century to study this type of chemistry. For example, the Gila monster has venom that helps control blood sugar. Gila monsters are binge eaters, so when they bite into a large meal, they release things in their venom that lower blood sugar. Because of chemistry, doctors figured out how to use this venom to lower blood sugar in diabetic patients.

If you are interested in chemistry, the best way to learn about all the different uses for chemistry is to have fun doing experiments. What's fun about doing chemistry experiments is that you get to see how chemicals react together to make something new. A great place to start is by making a volcano eruption out of baking soda. (Remember to always ask a parent first). You can also learn more about the snails that Dr. Mandë works with by playing the card game she developed called "Killer Snails: Assassins of the Sea" (find at www.killersnails.com) or search for "Dr. Mandë Holford, Killer Snail Ted Talk" to see a video of the snail eating a fish and learn more about her work.

75

Dream of Looking For Culture

LIKE

Susie Crate

Do you enjoy going on field trips? Usually this means you get to leave school for the day and go somewhere new to learn or have fun. In anthropology this is about understanding culture, simply defined as the way people think, what they do, and what they make that is shared and learned across generations. To study culture means going to a different place from where you came from or getting to know another group of people where you live. Susie Crate does this to understand different cultures different from her own.

When Susie went on a field trip to Kiribati, a remote island in the South Pacific, she observed a different community structure. People let the children roam free. It was everyone's job, not just their immediate family, to raise and protect the children. Do you think that would work where you live in America? It would probably be considered rude unless you lived in a special community who agreed to it.

Susie's focus as an anthropologist is to study one culture for a long time and to travel around the world and compare with others. One of the areas she studies is how climate change is affecting different cultures. Climate change is caused by humans and impacts our nature and weather. Susie believes that we know a lot about numbers that relate to our changing planet but that, "We are missing the human face of climate change." She wants people to learn from the cultures who are being impacted.

Susie has worked with one culture in Siberia, Russia for 30 years who herd cows and horses. Climate change is making the permafrost (frozen ground) thaw, turning hay fields into lakes while the land is rising and falling. Now they can't feed their animals.

In Kiribati (an island state in the middle of the ocean), Susie talked to people worried about sea-level rise. The rising waters threatened to flood their homes. They tried to build walls, but the sea still rises. One elder man told her, "The tide came in little by little and for the last 30 years washed away the houses and the trees beside them. When you see your land broken, there is a shaking in the heart."

Susie traveled to Peru to understand how the mountain glaciers were disappearing because of climate change. For thousands of years, farmers there have used the glacier water for their crops. But the glaciers are melting and soon will be gone. That means no food for the people or animals there.

Susie also visited a community in the United States to show that we are also being affected by climate change here. She talked to watermen, crab and oyster harvesters on the Chesapeake Bay in Virginia. They told her that because the ocean water is warmer now, they are trapping less and less.

Susie says that, "Anthropologists follow in the tradition of being activists. If you see injustice, you want to help these people get a voice." Susie speaks up for the people she studies. Some people deny climate change and global warming because stopping it requires humans to change their habits and take care of the planet. She would say, "We can't change the world, but we can change ourselves, which then, will change the world. I think it will be my daughters' generation that will have the gumption to turn it around."

Dream of Looking for Cures

LIKE

the Virus Ninja, Kizzmekia Corbet

Did you know that cells in your body have the ability to remember things? They do! While it might not be a ton of fun, it's the reason that your doctor encourages you to get shots to help fight certain sicknesses. A shot (or vaccination) is a dead or weakened form of the germ that is put into your body, causing your immune response to jump into action. It creates antibodies that remember this germ. Then if the real germ shows up in your body, it will be ready to fight it. It's like practicing karate. During practice your opponent is not out to harm you, but if a real enemy shows up, then you are ready for a real fight.

Over the course of history, many sicknesses like measles, mumps, and polio that were once very scary can be managed because enough people got vaccinations and stopped it from spreading. In the year 2020, the world was introduced to a sickness called "Covid-19."

During this time, Kizzmekia Corbet lead scientist at the National Institute of Health who research the creation of a Covid-19 vaccination.

When Kizzmekia was in 4th grade, her teacher knew that "Kizz" was special. She watched as she rushed to help other kids who were falling behind. Her teacher asked her parents to send her to a special school for bright children. Kizzmekia's parents were proud of their daughter and insisted that she find jobs in high school that would help her get a college scholarship. She took a job at a chemistry lab during her 10th grade summer. While other kids were out playing, she was learning. Her lab partner was a Black graduate student who taught her about becoming a doctor of science and the possibilities that a future in science could hold. For Kizzmekia seeing another person of color was inspiring, "He helped me realize how important and fun science was. It helped me see that being him was possible."

Long before COVID-19, Kizzmekia was studying coronaviridae, which is a family of related viruses. Her work focused on sicknesses in this family called SARS and MERS. The reason that COVID-19 has it's name is because when you pull it apart it means "*CO*rona"+ "*VI*rus"+ "*Disease*"+ "20*19*." This means it is in the same family of coronaviridae sicknesses that Kizzmekia has spent years studying.

Because she had a head start working on these other, related sicknesses, she was excited to help make a difference when COVID-19 appeared. She explained on a news program to the world how the vaccine would work, "The vaccine includes a 'spike protein,' which is the protein that is on the surface of the virus (the thing that makes you sick). That protein is the reason why the virus can attach to a cell, get into a cell, and cause an infection. The goal is to get that protein into a vaccine and allow the body to create antibodies. These antibodies would block an infection later."

Put another way, her job is to figure out how to take the part of COVID-19 that makes you sick and SAFELY introduce it to your body. This way, if the real virus shows up, your body already knows how to fight it. She is basically a virus ninja.

We will need more researchers like Kizzmekia from your generation to help ensure that if another sickness should rear its ugly head, that we have a troop of virus ninjas ready to help us fight it. A really important way that you can get involved now is to talk to someone who is a doctor or a science teacher to understand the REAL advantages and disadvantages of vaccinations, as not all information about vaccinations is accurate. This is a choice that you will need to make for yourself one day and the more you understand about the science, the better choice you can make. Understanding how vaccinations work can also help you explain how it works to others who may not understand the science.

Explaining to others is useful because if not enough people get the vaccination, it can keep continuing to spread. So, it is important that your family and friends understand the risks and rewards of getting vaccinations. Who knows, you may even help save a life!

Dream of Looking for Answers with Science

LIKE

Bill Nye

Why is the sky blue? Why can airplanes fly? Why do rainbows have so many colors? Are you the type of person who is constantly asking, "Why, why, why?" Many times, the questions you ask can be answered by science. We rely on science to help us understand the world around us. Scientists like Bill Nye help us understand science and how it impacts our lives. As the world continues to change, we count on looking to the younger generation to study and promote science and what it can teach us.

Bill Nye can remember the exact moment that he fell in love with science. He transferred from a school that did not have a good science program to a school that celebrated science. Bill and his friend were learning about the period of a pendulum which is the time required to complete each swing. They were taught the equation in class, but he wanted to see it work in real life. They got a rope and made a pendulum that hung from the ceiling. They worked the equation and then gave the pendulum a good swing. He couldn't believe it. It really worked. "It felt as though we had unlocked the mystery of the universe," said Bill. He took over part of his parents' basement and could frequently be found running science experiments and doing what he calls the "nerd mindset" by creating knowledge for the love of knowledge.

He loved science so much as a kid that he was disappointed as an adult to understand that not all kids felt the same way. No one was showing kids that science could be fun. Nye decided to create a TV show called *Bill Nye the Science Guy* for kids that helped explain science in a fun way and encouraged experimenting.

An example of this is an art project called marbling. Marbling is when you create swirls of color that look like stone patterns. What can marbling teach us about science? Well, did you know that the reason that oil spills are so bad is because oil and water do not mix and so the oil spreads easily and quickly through water? Marbling involves mixing oil, water and food color together and mixing them onto paper or fabric. You will see when you do this, that the colored water and oil stay separate, creating a marbled pattern, just like happens with oil spills in the ocean.

Many adults recognize Bill as the TV star who taught them science when they were kids. He decided to use his fame to take on science-based causes. Climate change is supported by a lot of scientific data, but not everyone believes that it is real. Bill helps people understand the data better. He even got a popular weatherman to change his mind and publish an article about how science swayed him. He also helps educate people about why vaccinations are so valuable. Bill believes that, "We are all nerds deep down and nerds don't give up. Nerds are driven to use tools of reason, combined with the very best information available to solve the biggest, most unsolvable looking problems. These skills are available to everyone. Everyone has an inner nerd just waiting to be awakened by the right passion."

Being a science advocate might sound like an unusual job description, but technology has helped create confusion around a lot of issues that impact your generation. People willing to help explain and educate are needed. You could be a teacher, an activist, a lobbyist, a writer, or a YouTube star. There are many ways that you can help science continue to be appreciated and understood.

81

Dream of Looking For Genetic Solutions

LIKE

Dr. Jean Bennett

Do you ever wonder why you or your siblings look like your mother or father? All of our features like hair color, eye color, and height are determined by something called DNA. Our DNA is a code inside of our body that is a combination of traits from our mother and father. Each piece of code is a gene, such as an eye color gene that determines what color eyes you have.

There are doctors who study these genes to better understand how we can use them to improve our heath, these doctors are called geneticist. Every year more than a million babies are born with diseases caused by a single error in our genes. Doctors, like Dr. Jean Bennett, are developing methods for fixing these errors and curing the diseases they cause.

One of the people that Dr. Bennett helped was named Molly. When Molly was young, she would stare at the lights around her with a unique fascination. However, the older she got, the more her parents realized that she was only focusing on the light. They took her to a doctor and learned that she had an error in one of her genes that causes blindness. She was losing her sight and so her family set out to figure out how to help her.

There are certain dogs that have this same type of genetic error as Molly. Dr. Bennett was studying how she might fix this error by studying these dogs. She helped develop a medication that could be put into the dog's eye that would find the one bad gene and fix it! It was such an amazing feeling when she gave this medication to a group of dogs and their owners began calling her to say, "my dog can see!"

Molly and her family learned about this medication and Molly wanted to be one of the first people to try it. Since all of her sight was not lost, she was able to still save it and even improve it. The treatment had been tested for 11 years and it was ready for trial. Molly received the gene therapy and as she opened her eyes for the first time afterwards, she looked up to see the moon and stars. It was one of the most beautiful things she had ever seen.

Dr. Bennett knows her work has a big impact on people, "Each time I hear reports about how this therapy has improved someone's life, it is a miracle to me. It could be the first approved gene therapy in the United States."

The current treatments can only slow blindness or slightly improve it, not cure total blindness, however, as more and more work is done, this type of disease and other genetic diseases have a chance of being cured. The medical research is increasing so young people are needed to join the field to continue to make progress.

If you are interested in the power of DNA, there are kits you can purchase, with the help of an adult, that help you learn more about your ancestors, where your family came from in the world and your own health. All from a code in your body that is so small you can't see it.

38

Dream of Looking for Patterns

LIKE

Hannah Fry

Do you have a music or movie app that you use like Netflix or Spotify? Do you notice that when you open the app, it suggests shows or music artists that you might like? It seems to have "learned" what you like and knows other things that you might like as a result. Your app learns about what you like by spotting patterns.

As you watch, you generate data about your preferences. The more you watch, the more patterns you create. It is just simple numbers about you. When a computer looks at that data and spots patterns, it can turn it into information that can be used to give you suggestions. Hannah Fry is a mathematician who helps spot patterns in data that are useful to society. She is the one who helps to tell the computer how to spot your movie-watching patterns.

Hannah, however, did not always like data, but she loved math. She loved math because of how neat and orderly it is and that equations could explain the world around her. Data is big and messy because it is just a lot of numbers without any order. She read about how a website designer used math to uncover a pattern and realized that working with data is like solving a puzzle with math, and Hannah loves puzzles.

The website designer discovered that if you go to any Wikipedia and click on the top link enough times, it always takes you to the philosophy page. Using Math, it was proven that this is true for 95% of Wikipedia pages. If this could be used for a silly website puzzle, she wondered, "What other patterns could help us better understand our cities, our health, our world and our lives?"

When Hannah studied the world around her, she found examples everywhere. She found a dairy farmer who had his cows wear pedometers to track their movement. By tracking the data of their movement and finding patterns, the farmer found that cows who were ready to have babies moved around a lot more than normal cows. Now, the farmer knows easily which cows are ready to have babies and on which days.

Hannah herself started collecting and conducting research about a topic that you would not think could be studied using math: love. She says that, "Love, as with most of life, is full of patterns."

She looked at patterns from a website where people are looking for new friends. The patterns showed that unique people made more friends. People who used pictures that played up their unique attributes, instead of just trying to fit in, were more likely to get messages from other people. She used math to prove that it is better to be yourself and be different. Hannah learned so much about love and friendship, through math, that she wrote a book called *The Mathematics of Love*.

Hannah is now a professor who studies patterns and works to make the world a better place by helping study crime and city living. She also hosts TV shows and radio programs and writes books about how the patterns in data can help us look at things in a new way.

If you are interested in learning more about finding patterns in data, Hannah is a great teacher. She hosts two shows, *The Joy of Data* and *The Joy of Winning*, that help explain these concepts and have fun examples of how to use these concepts in your every day life. If you look up "Hannah Fry Monopoly" on the Internet, you can also learn how to use math to beat your family in Monopoly!

39

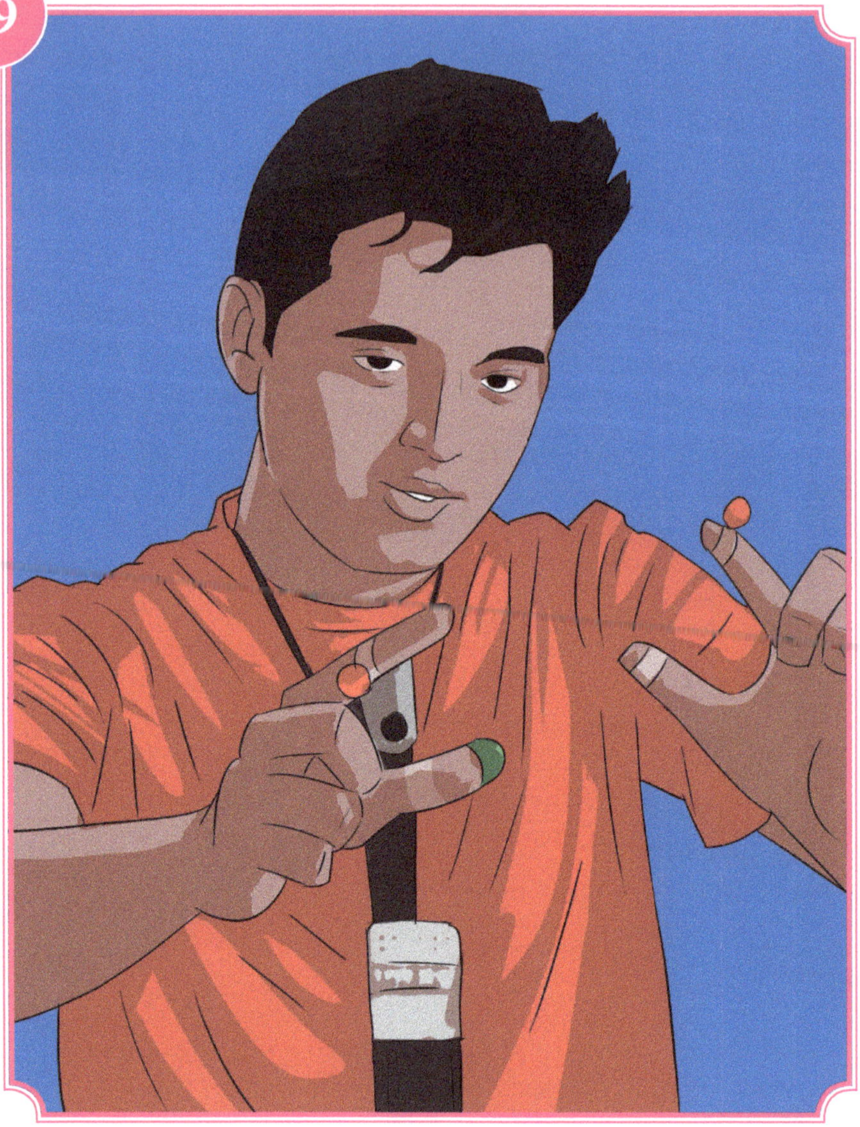

Dream of Looking For New Technology

LIKE

Pranav Mistry

The cartoon *The Jetsons* was created in 1962 and set 100 years into the future in the year 2062. Even though we have a ways to go to get to 2062, many of the technologies predicted in this show, now exist today like: video calling, tablet computers, a cleaning robot, smart watches, drones, holograms, and flat screen TV's. Computer scientists, like Pranav Mistry, made all of these things that were once just the dreaming's of a cartoon possible. We need scientists like this to help us research and unlock new technologies that will change the *next* 100 years.

For most of Pranav's life in India computers were not very common. That didn't matter. His friends say that he loved computers and built his own, which won first prize in his schools science fair. Even then, all his friends all thought he would be the "Bill Gates of India" when he grew up.

Pranav followed his love for computers to one of the top technology schools in America. There, he helped advance a technology called "sixth sense." This technology allows people to use hand gestures to control the technology stored inside of their phone. For example, if you want to take a picture on your phone, you hold up your hands and pretend to take a picture and your phone will register what you are doing. Without ever having to take your phone out of your pocket, it will take a picture.

With "sixth sense" you can dial a phone number from a projection on your wrist. You can point to your wrist and a watch will appear with the time. You can touch a piece of paper and take notes with your finger. "Sixth sense" works because Pranav designed a technology that you wear around your neck (or in other versions as a hat) that reads sensors on your fingers and then "talks" to your phone. He says, "Imagination is the only limit to this technology." He truly meant this because instead of keeping it to make money, he shared the technology with the world and allowed anyone to use it as they wanted.

After school, Pranav went to work with Samsung, the phone company. He helped develop a new technology that is now its own company called NEON. Gone are the days of needing to invent a make-believe friend. Now you can have one that feels like a real person. NEON is a virtual being, meaning it lives inside of your computer. It looks like a person and behaves like a person. He calls these virtual beings, "artificial humans." Imagine a world where you wake up and take a class online from an "artificial teacher" and then place a breakfast order from an "artificial waiter" and during your lunch break, take a workout class from an "artificial instructor."

It is still yet to be determined how these types of advanced technology will influence our lives, but it is certain that they will. Inventing and discovering new technology will be a huge part of what makes your generation different from your parents and from your children.

If you want to learn more about computer science, the Khan academy has 3 different courses on the topic and it is all free. While working in technology of the future requires a strong understanding of math and sciences, as Pranav would say, "The real challenge is how far you can take your imagination!"

Dream of Looking for True Stories

LIKE

Studs Terkel

It's important that we study our past because that is how future generations will learn from us and try not to repeat our mistakes. A historian often becomes an expert of a certain event or a period in time. People look to them to learn from their knowledge. Wars are a major event that are often studied by lots of different historians. Their learning can help us avoid wars in the future.

Studs Terkel has contributed to our understanding of history by capturing the stories of everyday people in the United States over the last 100 years. As a child, Stud's parents owned a hotel. He considers this hotel to be his "college." He loved books, but he thinks that, "It is the combination of book smart and street smart that made me who I am." Studs would listen to the stories that the hotel guests would tell as they socialized. He was fascinated by the stories of people from all over.

This fascination turned into a career writing the stories of everyday people or sharing them on his radio show, "I use a tape recorder, but my real tool is curiosity," he says. Studslistened to a lot of people's stories. He learned about things that impact our every day life.

It was the 1930s and a woman and her family lost everything they had. This was a period of time when a lot of people were losing their jobs and did not have much money. You may have heard of it being called, " the Great Depression." This woman lived during a time when Black families and white families were not treated the same. This woman and her family were hungry and did not have enough food to eat. This woman was white and the family that made sure they had food to eat was Black. This experience made her realize that it is the heart of people that matter, not their skin. Isn't this a lesson from history that we could benefit learning from?

Studs wrote multiple books about different periods of time, like the Great Depression or certain cities, like Chicago. He didn't have a point he was trying to make about them. He says, "I would just talk to people. I want to know how ordinary people feel." Their stories document what life was like during those times.

"One of the reasons that I think that these books are so important is that this history has been denied to the young. It's like we are suffering from national memory loss", Studs says, "There is no memory of yesterday. What was it like to be a kid in the 1930s during the Great Depression? To watch your father come home from working at the same company for 10 years with his tool chest on his shoulder and not be able to work, even when he wants to. What is it like to be a part of that family?"

Another book he wrote was called, *Working*, inspired by Richard Scarry's, *What people do all day*. He thought, "This is something we need to do for grownups." He interviewed people who did all sorts of different jobs and told their stories. These stories would eventually be turned into a musical!

If you are interested in learning more about history, the series *Who Was* is a series about historical figures. You can learn through their books or Netflix. It's a great way to learn about history through people, as Studs would like you to do.

DREAM

IT &

do it

100 POSSIBILITIES, STORIES, REAL-LIFE ROLE MODELS.

FOR GIRLS AND BOYS

INSPIRING ALL THE THINGS YOU CAN BE

HOLLY A. SHARP

www.ingramcontent.com/pod-product-compliance
Lightning Source LLC
Chambersburg PA
CBHW041036050726
47599CB00018B/1985